BLACK+DECKER ™

THE BOOK OF HOME HOW-TO

COMPLETE PHOTO GUIDE TO OUTDOOR BUILDING

Decks • Sheds • Garden Structures • Pathways

The Editors of Cool Springs Press

COOL SPRINGS PRESS

Brimming with creative inspiration, how-to projects, and useful information to enrich your everyday life, Quarto Knows is a favorite destination for those pursuing their interests and passions. Visit our site and dig deeper with our books into your area of interest: Quarto Creates, Quarto Cooks, Quarto Homes, Quarto Lives, Quarto Drives, Quarto Explores, Quarto Gifts, or Quarto Kids.

Inspiring | Educating | Creating | Entertaining

First Published in 2020 by Cool Springs Press, an imprint of The Quarto Group, 100 Cummings Center, Suite 265-D, Beverly, MA 01915, USA. T (978) 282-9590 F (978) 283-2742 QuartoKnows.com

Cool Springs Press titles are also available at discount for retail, wholesale, promotional, and bulk purchase. For details, contact the Special Sales Manager by email at specialsales@quarto.com or by mail at The Quarto Group, Attn: Special Sales Manager, 100 Cummings Center, Suite 265-D, Beverly, MA 01915, USA.

24 23 22 21 20   1 2 3 4 5

ISBN: 978-0-7603-6623-3

Digital edition published in 2020
eISBN: 978-0-7603-6624-0

Library of Congress Cataloging-in-Publication Data available.

Design & Page Layout: *tabula rasa* graphic design
Photography: Paul Markert (with assistance from Brad Holden, Ian Miller) pages 76 to 93; Rau + Barber (with assistance from Adam Esco) pages 124 to 141; Christopher Mills page 126; AZEK Building Projects pages 34, 35; Huettl Landscape Architecture page 14; Jerry Pavia pages 8, 64; Rich Fleischman (with assistance from Ian Miller and setbuilding by Brad Holden) pages 106 to 123; Shutterstock pages 48, 74

Black & Decker The Book of Home How-To Complete Photo Guide to Outdoor Building

Created by: The Editors of Cool Springs Press, in cooperation with BLACK+DECKER.

Printed in China

NOTICE TO READERS

For safety, use caution, care, and good judgment when following the procedures described in this book. The publisher and BLACK+DECKER cannot assume responsibility for any damage to property or injury to persons as a result of misuse of the information provided.

The techniques shown in this book are general techniques for various applications. In some instances, additional techniques not shown in this book may be required. Always follow manufacturers' instructions included with products, since deviating from the directions may void warranties. The projects in this book vary widely as to skill levels required: some may not be appropriate for all do-it-yourselfers, and some may require professional help.

Consult your local building department for information on building permits, codes, and other laws as they apply to your project.

CONTENTS

Building projects for your yard and garden is fun. You get to work outdoors. The materials are relatively easy to manage and the tolerances are a bit more forgiving than they are for indoor projects. And perhaps best of all, you get to see and enjoy the results quickly.

Outdoor building can be done with a wide array of materials, including exterior-rated wood, stone and masonry products, prefabricated panels such as fence panels and lattice, and even composite wood and plastic-based wood substitutes. Fasteners depend upon the type of material you are building with of course, but you will find many options for exterior-rated screws, nails, and wood hangers, as well as mortar for stonework. A basic tool kit that includes a circular saw, jigsaw, power miter saw and a drill-driver will get most carpentry jobs done. If you are building with stone or concrete, you can rent specialty tools for the job, including concrete mixers, plate compactors, wet saws for cutting pavers, and even earth moving equipment like skid-loaders for very ambitious tasks.

Finished projects made from wood can be painted, stained, clear-coated, or simply left unfinished to weather to pleasing gray tones is you are using natu-rally weather-resistant woods such as cedar, mahogany, and cypress. Concrete and stonework are usually left unfinished but in some cases, it makes sense to seal them to preserve their brand new look and make them easier to clean.

The projects featured in *BLACK+DECKER The Book of Home How-To Complete Photo Guide to Outdoor Building* represent a complete cross section of the types of projects we know to be the most popular for home DIYers. They include ground-level surfaces for entertaining and walking around; vertical elements like fences and walls; projects for entertaining and fun; and a few structures that employ techniques for sheds and outbuildings. They range from relatively easy to somewhat challenging. All are intended to be scalable, so you can adjust the dimensions to fit perfectly into your yard or garden.

Whichever materials you are interested in using and whatever forms you want them to take, we believe you will find your first forays into outdoor building to be satisfying and great way to build your own DIY skills. You will experience the pleasure of enjoying your new outdoor feature, and it will be even more enjoyable because you built it yourself.

WALKWAYS, PATIOS & DECKS

If you are taking a big-picture view of your yard and looking for a logical order to your projects, you probably will want to start with the flat living surfaces. These include patios, decks, walkways and, in some cases, steps. They are the infrastructure of your backyard, and you should prioritize them when it comes to assigning space.

With the exception of wood decks, it is difficult to avoid stone and concrete when you are creating a patio or a walkway. That's okay: these materials are relatively easy to work with and they can last for generations. They do require some physical effort, so be sure to factor that into your planning. A natural flagstone patio is a thing of beauty, but he individual flags can weigh 100 pounds or more so be sure to have some help lined up, be it other people or mechanical assistance such as a come-along.

Most of the stone-based projects you will find in this chapter involve a two-layer subbase. The first layer is usually compacted gravel that stabilizes the patio or walkway. This layer is normally made with compactible gravel that includes fines to bind the compacted, angular rock together into a solid surface. However, many homeowners these days are selecting to install a permeable subbase that allows water to drain through, instead of running off the surface and into the street or gutter. The only real difference between permeable and nonpermeable subbases is that a permeable base does not include the fines that knit everything together. The result is slightly less stable than a base made with traditional Class V–type gravel, but it is a distinctly greener approach that you will appreciate, especially if you live in an area with water scarcity.

Wood deckbuilding is a very popular DIY pursuit, and you will find many newer products that greatly simplify the joinery required. In this chapter we have featured only freestanding deck projects that can be installed anywhere in your yard. Decks that are attached to your home are not that much more difficult to create, but they are subject to many more building codes. And because they are attached to your house, they may not make the best option for your first outdoor building project. If you are interested in building an attached wood deck, we suggest you obtain a how-to book that is dedicated to these projects, such as *BLACK+DECKER The Complete Guide to Decks*.

NOTE: Before beginning any excavation, call 811 to make arrangements for having your utility lines flagged. This a free service and a very important step in making certain you do not accidentally cut into gas, water, or other utility lines.

LOOSE ROCK LANDSCAPE PATH

Loose materials can be used as filler between solid surface materials, like flagstone, or laid as the primary ground cover, as seen here.

oose-fill rock pathways are perfect for casual yards and other situations where a hard surface is not required. The material is inexpensive, easy to install, and its fluidity accommodates curves and irregular edging. For visual appeal, loose-rock paths may be matched to larger stones in the environment, tying them in to your landscaping.

For a more stable path, choose angular or jagged gravel instead of round rock. It knits together as it compresses, which makes it more level and firm. However, if your preference is to stroll through your landscape barefoot, your feet will be better served with smoother stones, such as river rock or pond pebbles with a diameter of ¾" or less. If it complements your landscaping,

use light-colored gravel, such as buff limestone. Visually, it is much easier to follow a light-colored pathway at night.

Stable edging helps keep the pathway gravel from migrating into the surrounding mulch and soil. When integrated with landscape fabric, the edging also keeps invasive plants from rooting in the pathway. Do not install gravel paths near plants and trees that produce messy fruits, seeds, or other debris that will be difficult to remove from the gravel. Organic matter left on gravel paths will eventually rot into compost that will support weed growth. A base of compactable gravel under the surface material keeps the pathway firm underfoot.

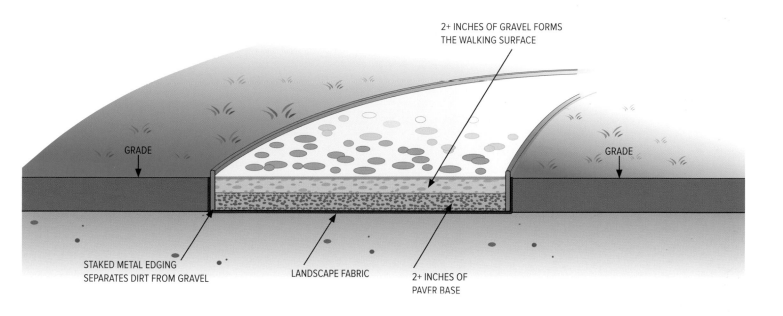

2+ INCHES OF GRAVEL FORMS
THE WALKING SURFACE

GRADE

GRADE

STAKED METAL EDGING
SEPARATES DIRT FROM GRAVEL

LANDSCAPE FABRIC

2+ INCHES OF
PAVER BASE

TOOLS & MATERIALS

Mason's string

Hose or rope

Marking paint

Excavation tools

Garden rake

Rubber mallet

Plate compactor (optional)

Sod cutter (optional)

Wood stakes

Lumber (1 × 2, 2 × 4)

Straight 2 × 4

Edging

Galvanized spikes

Professional-grade landscape fabric

Compactable gravel

Dressed gravel

Eye and ear protection

Work gloves

Circular saw

Maul

MAKE A SPACER GAUGE
To ensure that the edges of the pathway are parallel, create a spacer guide to install the edging. Use a piece of 2 × 4 that's a bit longer than the path width. At one end, cut a notch that will fit snugly over the edging. Cut another notch so the distance from the first notch to the other notch is the planned width of the pathway.

How to Make a Loose-Rock Landscape Path

Lay out one edge of the path excavation. Use a section of hose or rope to create curves, and use stakes and string to indicate straight sections. Cut 1 × 2 spacers to set the path width and establish the second pathway edge; use another hose and/or more stakes and string to lay out the other edge. Mark both edges with marking paint.

Remove sod in the walkway area using a sod stripper or a power sod cutter. Excavate the soil to a depth of 4 to 6". Measure down from a 2 × 4 placed across the path bed to fine-tune the excavation. Grade the bottom of the excavation flat using a garden rake. *Note: If mulch will be used outside the path, make the excavation shallower by the depth of the mulch.* Compact the soil with a plate compactor or tamper.

Lay landscaping fabric from edge to edge, lapping over the undisturbed ground on either side of the path. On straight sections, you may be able to run parallel to the path with a single strip; on curved paths, it's easier to lay the fabric perpendicular to the path. Overlap all seams by 6".

Install edging over the fabric. The top edge should be ½" above grade if the path passes through grass or 2" above grade if it passes through a mulched area. Secure the edging with spikes. To install the second edge, use a 2 × 4 spacer gauge that's been notched to fit over your edging.

Stone or vertical-brick edges may be set in deeper trenches at the sides of the path. Place these on top of the fabric also. You do not have to use additional edging with paver edging, but metal (or other) edging will keep the pavers from wandering.

Trim excess fabric, then backfill behind the edging with dirt and tamp it down with the end of a 2 × 4. This secures the edging and helps it to maintain its shape.

7

Add a 2- to 4"-thick layer of compactable gravel over the entire pathway. Rake the gravel flat. Then, spread a thin layer of your surface material over the base gravel.

8

Tamp the base and surface gravel together using a plate compactor. Be careful not to disturb or damage the edging with the compactor.

9

Fill in the pathway with the remaining surface gravel. Drag a 2 × 4 across the tops of the edging using a sawing motion, to level the gravel flush with the edging.

10

Set the edging brick flush with the gravel using a mallet and 2 × 4.

11

Tamp the surface again using the plate compactor or a hand tamper. Compact the gravel so it is slightly below the top of the edging. This will help keep the gravel from migrating out of the path. Rinse off the pathway with a hose to wash off dirt and dust and bring out the true colors of the materials.

STEPPING STONE LANDSCAPE PATH

A stepping stone path is both a practical and appealing way to traverse a landscape. With large stones as foot landings, you are free to use pretty much any type of fill material in between.

Stepping stones in a path serve two purposes: they lead the eye, and they carry the traveler. In both cases, the goal is rarely fast, direct transport, but more of a relaxing stroll that's comfortable, slow paced, and above all, natural.

Sometimes steppers are placed more for visual effect, with the knowledge that their primary goal is to be artful clusters of stones. Clustering is also an effective way to slow or congregate walkers near a fork in the path or at a good vantage point for a striking feature of the garden.

In the project featured here, landscape edging is used to contain the loose infill material (small aggregate); however a stepping stone path can also be effective without edging. For example, setting a series of steppers directly into your lawn and letting the lawn grass grow between them is a great choice as well.

Stepping stones blend beautifully into many types of landscaping, including rock gardens, ponds, flower or vegetable gardens, or manicured grass lawns.

Mason's string

Hose or rope

Marking paint

Sod stripper

Excavation tools

Hand tamper

Wood stakes

Lumber 1 × 2

Straight 2 × 4

Edging

Landscape fabric

Thick steppers or broad river rocks with one flat face

Coarse sand (optional)

½" to ½" pond pebbles (optional)

2½"-dia. river rock (optional)

Eye and ear protection

Work gloves

Level

Rake

CHOOSING STEPPERS

Select beefy stones (minimum 2½" to 3½" thick) with at least one flat side for use as stepping stones. Thinner stepping stones tend to sink into the pebble infill. Stones that are described as stepping stones usually have two flat faces. For the desired visual effect on this project, we chose steppers and 12"- to 24"- wide fieldstones with one broad, flat face.

CUTTING STEPPING STONES

You can make a stepping stone path without ever having to cut a stone, but if your design ideas are more directed toward straight edges than random, you can use a 2" or larger cold chisel and a mallet to strike off irregularities in your stones. You'll get a cleaner break if you score first with a masonry blade in your circular saw.

How to Make a Stepping Stone Landscape Path

Excavate and prepare a bed that's at least 4" deep. Use coarse building sand or paver base instead of compactable gravel for the base layer. Screed the sand flat (see page 22, step 6) so it's 2" below the top of the edging (depending on the thickness of your steppers—you want the stone surface to be ½" or so higher than the surrounding lawn surface). Do not tamp the sand.

Moisten the sand bed, then position the stepping stones in the sand, spacing them for comfortable walking and the desired appearance. As you work, place a 2 × 4 across three or more adjacent stones to make sure they are level with one another. Add or remove sand beneath the steppers, as needed, to stabilize and level the stones. Fill out your pathway, cutting irregularities off of your steppers as you see fit.

Pour in a layer of larger infill stones (2 ½"-dia. river rock is seen here). Smooth the stones with a garden rake. The infill should be below the tops of the stepping stones. Reserve about ⅓ of the larger diameter rocks.

4

Add the smaller infill stones that will migrate down and fill in around the larger infill rocks. To help settle the rocks, you can tamp lightly with a hand tamper, but don't get too aggressive— the larger rocks might fracture. Scatter the remaining large infill stones across the infill area (inset photo) so they float on top of the other stones.

SAND-SET PAVER PATIO

Brick pavers set in sand create a classic patio surface that's more casual than mortared pavers. The inherent flexibility of the sand-set finish allows for easy repair and maintenance or changes in the design. It also allows good drainage.

Brick or concrete pavers set in sand make for one of the simplest yet most rewarding and most forgiving patio projects. The installation process is straightforward and, because there's no mortar involved, you can complete the work at your own pace. Plus, as the freeze-thaw cycle and other forces inevitably cause some shifting, it is simple to maintain the patio simply by adding or removing sand from beneath the individual pavers.

Square-edged patios require fewer cuts and thus less time than curved designs. But if you want something out of the ordinary, sand-set brick is a good material to work with—the small units are perfect for making curves and custom features; even if you have a lot of cuts, you can make them quickly and accurately with a rented masonry wet saw.

To pave with any of the classic patterns, such as running bond or herringbone, you'll start at one corner of your patio border or edging. To ensure accurate layout, check that the sides of the edging form a 90-degree angle at the starting corner. If you're not using edging or any kind of formal border, set up mason's strings to guide the brick placement.

CUTTING PAVERS & BRICKS

If your design requires cuts, use a masonry wet saw (tub saw). These water-lubricated cutting tools are available for rent at most building centers and stone yards.

TOOLS & MATERIALS

Tape measure

Circular saw

Drill

Excavation tools

Mason's string

Stakes

Line level

Plate compactor or hand tamper

4-foot level

Rubber mallet

Push broom

Pavers

Lumber (2 × 2, 2 × 4)

2½" drywall screws

Compactable gravel

Work gloves

Professional-grade landscape fabric

U-shaped wire stakes (optional)

Rigid paver edging or other edging material

Lengths of 1" metal conduit

Coarse sand or paver base

⅛" hardboard strips

Plywood scrap

Paver joint sand

Rake

Trowel

Masonry wet saw

Eye and ear protection

Maul

Galvanized spikes

A sturdy base will help keep your sand-set patio from heaving due to the nature of outdoor building. This cross section shows the important elements of a good base, including a thick layer of subbase, landscape fabric, and a layer of coarse sand or paver base.

How to Lay Out Your Project Site

Set up batterboards and layout strings in a square or rectangle that's about 1 foot larger than the excavation area. Check to make sure the string layout is square, and set the strings

to follow a ⅛" per foot downward slope in the desired direction using a line level for guidance. Mark the excavation corners with stakes. The edges of the excavation should extend

about 6" beyond the finished patio footprint. Remove all sod and vegetation inside the area, reserving healthy sod for patching in around the finished patio.

How to Build a Sand-Set Paver Patio

Excavate the area to a depth that allows for a 6"-thick gravel subbase, a 1" layer of sand, and the paver thickness; account for the desired height of the finished surface above the surrounding ground. Use cross strings and a story pole to check the depth as you work.

Add an even 3" to 4" layer of compactable gravel over the entire site, and then tamp with a plate compactor or a hand tamper.

3

Install a layer of high-quality landscape fabric. Overlap rows of fabric by at least 6". If desired, pin the fabric in place with U-shaped wire stakes.

4

Install paver edging along two adjacent sides of the patio area, creating a perfect 90-degree corner. Trim the fabric along the back of the edging. Lay down lengths of 1"-dia. pipe in parallel lines about 3 to 6 feet apart.

5

Add a 1"-thick layer of coarse sand. Smooth it out with a rake so it just covers the pipes. Dampen the sand with water, then pack it down lightly with a hand tamper.

6

Screed the sand perfectly flat using a straight, long 2 × 4: rest the board on top of the pipes, and pull it backward with a side-to-side sawing motion. Fill in low spots with sand as you work. Dampen, tamp, and screed the sand again until the surface is smooth and flat and firmly packed. Remove the pipe(s) in the area where you will begin the paving. Fill the depression left by the pipe with sand, and then smooth it out with a short board or a trowel.

7

Begin setting the border bricks, starting at the right-angle corner of the patio edging, using ⅛" hardboard spacers if necessary. Complete the border row that will be parallel to the first course of field brick, and continue several feet up the perpendicular side edge.

8

FIELD UNITS

BORDER UNITS

Set the first course of field brick. These bricks should be centered over the sand joints of the completed border row. Use a mason's string tied between two bricks to align the leading edges of the first-course bricks. After setting several bricks, tap them with a rubber mallet to bed them into the sand layer. Complete the first field course, and then add some border units along the edge.

9

Snug a piece of edging against the installed brick and anchor it in place. *Note: Install the remaining edging as the paving progresses*. Continue setting the brick using the mason's string and spacers for consistent spacing and alignment.

10

Check each 4-foot section for level to make sure the bricks are even across the top. Remove low or high bricks and add or remove sand beneath to bring them flush with the surrounding bricks. Work atop a plywood platform to prevent displacing the bricks. Complete the paving.

11

Spread paver sand over the surface, then sweep the sand to fill the joints. Sweep the surface clean. Compact the surface and joints with a plate compactor or hand tamper, and then fill the joints one or more times until they are completely filled after compaction. Sweep up any loose sand. Soak the surface with water and let it dry. If necessary, fill and tamp again, then hose off the surface and let it dry.

VARIATION: If your patio design includes curves or rounded corners, mark bricks for cutting curves by holding each brick in position and marking the desired cutting line onto the top face, then make the cuts with a masonry saw.

PERMEABLE SUBBASE

Patios made with rock or masonry units should have a stable subbase of compacted rock or gravel, usually beneath a layer of coarse sand into which the surfacing materials are set. Typically, these subbase layers are 6 to 8 inches thick, depending on your soil conditions—loose, loamy, or sandy soil needs a thicker subbase. A standard subbase made from compactable gravel (called Class II or Class V in most areas) hardens to form a solid mass when it is compacted. Water runoff will not penetrate such a subbase. Patio builders have begun to recognize a higher demand for water retention and for minimizing runoff, and they have developed permeable subbases that stabilize the patio, while still allowing water to seep through into the subsoil below instead of running off and into the wastewater collection system.

The key to a permeable subbase is called "open-grade" drainage rock. Where Class II and Class V are sifted with fine pulverized material (usually limestone) that hardens, ungraded drainage rock is just a rock. Most landscape-material stores carry it in two sizes: ¾-inch aggregate and 1- to ½-inch aggregate. The prevailing wisdom suggests placing a layer of the larger rock first, compacting it, and then topping it off with a compacted layer of the smaller drainage rock before you put down your sand bed (if you are using one). Once you've created a permeable subbase, it will look and function very much like a traditional subbase.

A permeable subbase is of little value if you top it with an impermeable or minimally permeable surfacing, such as interlocking pavers. Use either material that allows water to drain through it (such as pervious pavers), or install impermeable materials with large enough gaps between the individual members that the water will run off and drain through the gaps.

A permeable subbase looks like a typical compacted gravel subbase, but because the open-grade drainage rock is devoid of fines, it does not form a solid layer and thus it allows water to run through, not off.

TOOLS & MATERIALS

Stakes and mason's line

Tape measure

Maul

Shovels and other excavation tools

Wheelbarrow

Hand tamper

Landscape rake

Plate compactor (optional)

Level

Ear and eye protection

Large (1½" diameter) open-grade drainage rock

Smaller (¾" diameter) open-grade rock

Landscape fabric or geogrid textile (optional)

Edging

Coarse sand or pulverized granite (optional)

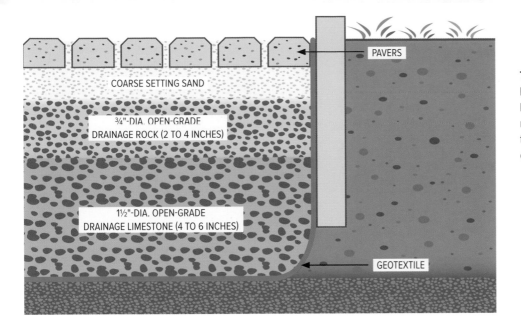

COARSE SETTING SAND

¾"-DIA. OPEN-GRADE
DRAINAGE ROCK (2 TO 4 INCHES)

1½"-DIA. OPEN-GRADE
DRAINAGE LIMESTONE (4 TO 6 INCHES)

PAVERS

GEOTEXTILE

The building blocks of a permeable subbase look a lot like a traditional paving subbase. The big difference is that a permeable base does not include fines, which are granular particles that knit together and create a layer that water cannot penetrate.

The components of a permeable subbase, from bottom to top, include a 4" to 6" layer of 1½"-diameter open-grade drainage rock (A) (limestone is shown here); above that, a 2" to 4" layer of ¾" open-grade drainage rock (B); a top layer of coarse sand (C) or pulverized granite for use as a setting bed for flagstone or masonry units.

How to Install a Permeable Subbase

1

MINIMUM SLOPE:
½" PER 10 FEET
AWAY FROM HOUSE

LINE LEVEL

Drive corner stakes with a maul and outline the patio area. Run mason's lines between the corner stakes. Ideally, the patio should slope away from an adjoining house at a rate of around ½" for every 10 feet. Set a level line along the edges of the patio perpendicular to the house. Adjust the line downward to create the ¼" per 1-foot slope.

2

STORY POLE

Begin excavating the site. A typical permeable subbase is 8" below grade when you allow for the thickness of the setting layer and the pavers or other surfacing. Use your layout strings to establish your digging depth. Measure the distance from the mason's line to the ground and add the depth of your excavation—8" in the project seen here. Make a story pole with markings that match the distance from the planned bottom of the excavation to the mason's line. Keep the lines in place as you dig (this does create an obstacle but it is the best way to assure that you don't overdig).

3

Excavate the patio site using the story pole as a depth guide. Be sure to call (in the US, simply dial 811) and have any utility lines flagged before you begin digging. Be careful not to dig too deeply, as the best base for your subbase is undisturbed earth. Once the excavation is complete, remove the strings and prepare for the installation of the subbase.

4

A permeable base is made with open-grade rock, which is simply landscape rock that has no fines or binders, as typical subbase (often called Class II or Class V) does. The bottom layer should be rock that is not smooth and has a diameter of 1½" to 2". Spread a 2"- to 4"-deep layer of rock over the excavation area.

5

Spread the rock out into an even layer. Use a garden rake or landscape rake to spread it. The subbase should extend past the planned edges of the project area by at least 10" on all open sides.

6

Tamp the rock to compact it. You can use a hand tamper, but for best results use a rented plate compactor. This is a very important part of creating a solid patio base, so be sure to be diligent with your efforts. Compact the rock as you go, and do not compact more than 2" of material at one time. Wear foam ear plugs or other ear protection. Add additional layers of large rock until the base layer is at least 4" thick. Then, switch to a smaller open-grade rock for the next layer. Here, ¾"-dia. buff limestone is being used. Add, spread, and compact the smaller-grade rock until the leveled surface follows the grade of the patio and the surface of the rock layer is 2", plus the thickness of your surfacing material, below grade at the top of the worksite. Add a sand-setting layer and pavers according to the demands of your project.

SPACED MASONRY PAVERS

Larger gaps between pavers, coupled with a permeable subbase, allow for a patio that lets water drain down instead of running off.

A bit of space between each paver is all it takes to turn a mostly impervious surface like masonry pavers into something that replenishes groundwater and spares storm drains. You have several options for building these earth-friendly gaps into your project:

- **Spaced conventional pavers.** Boost the earth friendliness of standard concrete pavers or bricks by installing them with gaps between them. Fill the gaps with river rock or creeping plants.
- **Mounting grids.** Plastic mounting grids not only lock in pavers a consistent space from each other, they help keep the installation smooth and level.
- **Pavers with preformed spacers.** Some pavers come with small nubs that separate them just enough to allow for drainage. They install as quickly and easily as conventional pavers, although the effectiveness is reduced by the narrowness of the gaps.

For this project, you'll also need to prepare a deep substrate of coarse, angular gravel to handle the water. Your soil type will dictate its depth. At the extreme, you may have to excavate 10 to 12 inches to make room for 8 inches of ¾- to 1½-inch open-graded stone (See pages 24 to 27), followed by at least 2 inches of coarse sand or screenings as a setting bed.

The project that follows uses widely spaced 16-inch by 16-inch pavers. One advantage of large pavers is that they look best if laid out so only whole pieces are used. No cutting! Once the substrate and edging are in place, use spacers and a taut line to install the pavers.

TOOLS & MATERIALS

Safety glasses, gloves, ear protection

Tape measure

Circular saw

Hammer

Drill-driver, bits

Excavation tools

Stakes

Mason's string

Line level

Plate compactor

Rubber mallet

Rake

Trowel

Lengths of 1" metal conduit

Rigid paver edging

Galvanized spikes

Scrap plywood and 2 × 2 for making spacers

¾" to 1½" open-grade stone for base

Coarse sand or screenings for setting bed

Pea gravel, river rock, crushed granite, or sand to fill gaps

Topsoil and plants (if adding plants)

The 16" × 16" wet-cast concrete pavers would shed rainwater and runoff if they were butted against one another in the traditional manner.

By leaving a 3" gap filled with pulverized granite, you create a route for water to soak into the permeable subbase and subsoil.

USING SPACERS

One of the least expensive ways to make an earth-friendly patio is to install conventional pavers with extra space between them for drainage. Any amount of spacing helps, whether a mere ¼-inch gap filled with coarse sand or 3 inches or more for stone or plantings. The consistent geometry of conventional pavers makes it relatively easy to achieve straight courses. However, once you introduce a gap you'll need to contrive spacers to help keep the gap consistent and the pavers neatly lined up. Guides can range from a few strips of ¼-inch hardboard to 2 × 2 and plywood combinations made to suit your arrangement.

Simple strips of ¼" hardboard or plywood work fine as gap guides. Adding a scrap of 1 × 2 makes them easier to use. Make several so they are always handy. This relatively small gap works well with smaller cast concrete pavers similar in size to brick pavers.

For a 1½" gap, use a 2 × 2 as a spacer. Adding a scrap of ½" plywood to ride on the paver tops makes the spacer easier to handle and helps you level adjacent pavers. This spacing is good with medium-sized pavers, such as these 8 × 16 concrete pavers.

To install a grid of square pavers, make a cross spacer about 16" by 16". Two 2 × 2s gives you a roughly 3-inch gap without having to rip a 2 × 4. Add the cross made of ¼" to ¾" plywood to match to the thickness of the pavers and hold the 2 × 2s together. For ease of use, attach a 1 × 2 handle. This is the spacer used for the featured project to follow, which uses large 16" × 16" pavers.

How to Install a Spaced-Paver Patio

1

Prepare a permeable subbase that extends at least 10" past the planned borders of the patio, where possible. Install rigid paver edging around the border of the patio area to contain the coarse sand or crushed-granite setting base material.

2

Embed 1"-dia. pieces of conduit into the sand at 4- to 6-foot intervals, making sure the conduit pieces are flush with one another and follow the slope you want to build into the patio. Screed using a piece of straight 2 × 4 over the conduit to level the paver setting medium. Slowly move the 2 × 4 back and forth in a sawing motion. Avoid walking on the setting bed once it is smooth. Remove the conduit and backfill the depressions.

3

Lay a setting bed that is at least 2" thick on top of the subbase. Level the setting bed. Do not use a power plate compactor on this bed, as it will make adjusting the pavers very difficult. It is okay to use a hand tamper to level and lightly compact the material.

4

Starting at a corner, set four tiles, using a cross spacer (see previous page) to position the pavers. *Note: When using spacers to lay out a patio next to a house, always start at the house and work outward. In cases where you are working in a closed corner, choose that corner to start. That way, if the corner is slightly out of square, which is common, you can make it up at the open sides of the patio where it is less noticeable.*

5

Continue to set pavers onto the setting bed, fanning outward from the corner where you started. Rely on the spacer to position the pavers, and go back to recheck the gaps as you work. For best results, make many spacers and leave them in place as you work.

6

Once you've set several pavers, check to make sure you are staying level. Lay a straight 2 × 4 across the tops and look for gaps between the straightedge and the pavers.

7

Add or remove bedding base from beneath the pavers as needed to bring them to level. Use some restraint here, as it is very easy to throw off your layout by adding too much bedding.

8

Use a **rubber mallet** and a scrap of 2 × 4 to adjust misaligned pavers. Again, use restraint here and be mindful of the lines formed by the grid pattern. Even slight deviations will show up very clearly.

9

Place all the pavers, then add filler between the pavers. Here, the same crushed (also called composted) granite that was used for the setting base is used to fill in the gaps. Keep a supply of the material around, as it is likely you'll need to refresh it from time to time as the level gets lower.

Option: Fill the spaces between the pavers with topsoil or potting soil so you can add attractive groundcover plants that don't mind being underfoot. Some may even add a pleasant fragrance as you walk across them. For areas with full sun, consider creeping thyme or elfin thyme. In partial sun, goldmoss sedum, chamomile, dichondra, and Irish moss work well. In shady areas, go with Corsican sandwort or sweet woodruff. Or, simply plant grass.

COMPOSITE PERMEABLE PAVERS

These pavers are not permeable themselves (as some are), but they are placed in installation grids that allow water to pass through. The pavers seen here are relatively thin and can be installed in their grids directly onto an existing patio surface, or they can be set onto a paver base as traditional sand-set masonry units.

nstalling composite permeable pavers is a doubly conscientious way to surface your patio. Not only are you limiting runoff, you are saving energy by using pavers made mostly of scrap tires and plastics. The recycled materials keep the pavers light and easy to cut. In addition, installation is simplified because the pieces snap into a plastic grid—no bond line, setting, and resetting required. Patterns include herringbone, basket weave, or running bond. Wedge-shaped accessory pavers let you install curved borders.

As with any permeable material, you'll need to excavate deeply and add coarse gravel for adequate drainage. For a patio, dig down about 12 inches. Begin with a 6-inch layer of 2½-inch stone, compacted 2 inches at a time. Next add a 4-inch layer of 1-inch stone, topped off with a 2-inch bedding layer of ⅜-inch chip rock. Slope the final layers away from the house.

Before installation, choose a starting point. To give your project a squared-up start and reduce the amount of cutting you'll have to do, look for a corner on the longest straight edge.

TOOLS & MATERIALS

Safety glasses, gloves, ear protection

Shovel

Hand dolly

Broom

Straightedge or screed rake

Hand trowel

Hammer

Tin snips

Utility knife

Edging and 10" spikes

4-foot level

Hand compactor or vibrating plate compactor

Jigsaw

Power miter saw (optional)

¾- to 1½-inch open-grade stone for base

Coarse sand or screenings for setting bed

Pavers and setting grids

Legless and wedge pavers for curved border

Caulk gun and exterior adhesive

The installation grids on which these pavers are fitted allow water runoff to drain into the subbase as it filters down through the gaps between the composite paver units.

In general, recycled composite products weigh less than solid stone or wood, and because the size is uniform they can be laid in traditional paver patterns like basket weave or herringbone. The VAST pavers seen here (see Resources, page 143) come in five colors so you can incorporate color shifts into the layout pattern.

How to Install Composite Pavers

Create a smooth base for the installation as you would for a standard paver installation project. If you are working next to a concrete surface, notch a 2 × 4 so the thickness equals the height of the paver plus the grid and use the 2 × 4 to screed the setting layer smooth once it is compacted. Unlike sandset pavers, this product installs better if the base is compacted hard and smooth.

Lay out several grids on the bedding layer. These rest on the bedding layer and are held together by installing the pavers so they bridge the joints between the grids. Plan how to begin your pattern of choice—herringbone, basket weave, or running bond—so that at least one paver overlaps two grids in each direction.

Install the pavers, beginning in one corner and working across one side of the patio. Often the side along the house works best for starting to avoid having to cut too many pavers. Complete the field of the patio. Here, a basket weave pattern is being used. One advantage to the basket weave, compared to herringbone (inset), is that the basket weave does not require half-size pavers.

Use a charged hose (one with the water turned on but the sprayer off) to mark a curved edge, if your design calls for one. Lay out the curve and carefully mark it for cutting.

5

Cut the curved edge with a jigsaw equipped with a coarse blade set just deep enough to cut through the pavers. You may need to attach a guide block to the foot of the saw to avoid cutting into the grids. But you can also cut the grids in place at the same time if you wish. Or, simply leave them and cover them with backfill. Note that any whole unused pavers can be easily lifted out and used elsewhere.

6

7

Use wedge-shaped pavers to create a decorative border treatment for the curve. Dry-fit the edge pavers first, since they are legless and do not lock into the installation grid. When satisfied, remove each piece. Add beads of landscape block adhesive and reset the border pieces. Complete any straight edges in the same manner. Check with the product manufacturer first to see if they recommend a specific brand or type of adhesive.

Add edging, securing it with 10" galvanized spikes every foot or so. Trim the grid with a jigsaw or cover it with soil and turf. If you wish, sweep chip rock onto the surface before tamping the entire surface. Sweep additional rock into the cracks as you tamp. Chip rock, also called pulverized or decomposed granite, will fill the gaps and stabilize the surface without blocking water drainage.

BOARDWALK DECK ON A SLAB

There's no need to let a cracked, aging concrete patio ruin the look and enjoyment of your backyard. Instead of breaking it up and removing it, build a very simple deck platform right over the old slab. The result will be a beautiful new outdoor platform that improves the look of the home and the yard, as well as the accessibility.

This is an independent deck; the structure is not attached to the house, but is instead laid atop the slab and allowed to move with any shifting in the concrete. It's constructed on a simple frame base laid level with sleepers over the concrete itself. This means that the deck will be very close to the ground and subject to a great deal of moisture. Only certain types of decking will tolerate those conditions. We've used pressure-treated pine deckboards.

The design of the deck is a plain rectangle and can easily be constructed over a weekend. We've spruced up the look a bit by laying the decking in a herringbone pattern. More complex patterns would make the deck surface look even more impressive—just remember to do yourself a favor and work the patterns out before cutting any decking.

Turn a boring or failing concrete slab into an attractive walkout or entertainment space with a short utility, or boardwalk, deck installed on top of it.

TOOLS & MATERIALS

2" and 3" deck screws

Composite or plastic shims

Circular saw

Miter saw

Power drill and bits

Treated lumber (2 × 4, 2 × 2)

Caulk gun and glue

Level

Chalk line

Stain

Work gloves

Eye and ear protection

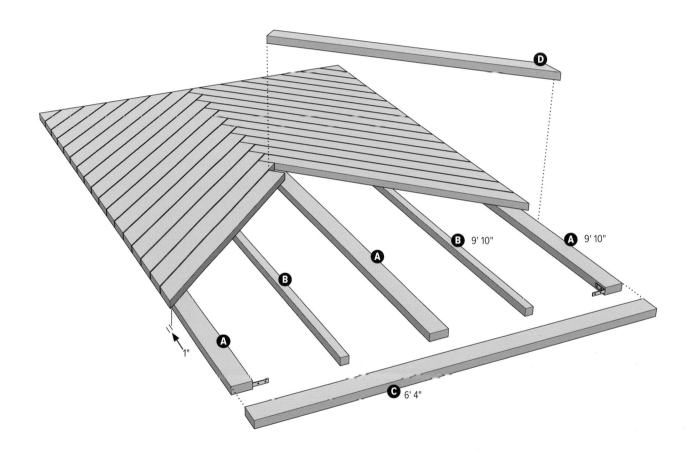

CUTTING LIST

KEY	QUANTITY	SIZE	PART	MATERIAL
A	3	1½ × 3½ × 128"	Frame side	PT pine
B	2	1½ × 1½ × 128"	Nailer	PT pine
C	2	1½ × 3½ × 76"	Frame end	PT pine
D	60	1½ × 3½ × (cut to fit)	Decking	PT pine

How to Build a Boardwalk Deck

Build and assemble the frame offsite by cutting and measuring 10-feet 2 × 4s to length and securing them together with galvanized metal corner brackets.

Install the nailer joists by measuring and cutting parallel boards to the length of the frame. Use 2" deck screws and galvanized metal corner brackets to secure the nailer joists to the frame.

Clear away any dust and debris from the concrete slab. Set the frame atop the slab and use 8" plastic shims to level it. Glue shims in place and cut off excess so shims are flush with the frame.

Use a level as you work with the shims to ensure an even plane on which to build the deck.

5

Remove the frame from the slab before installing the decking. Stagger the 2 × 4s in a crosshatch pattern in opposing 45-degree angles from the center nailing joist. Attach the boardwalk pattern to the frame using 3" deck screws. Boards should abut one another along the length of the joist and allow for at least 1" of overhang from the frame.

6

Mark 1" overhang on all sides of the frame using a chalk line, and cut off excess decking using a circular saw equipped with a carbide blade.

7

Use a helper to install the decking atop the concrete slab, checking for level and using shims to adjust as necessary.

8

Clear away dust and debris and stain the decking as desired.

FLOATING DECK

A full-size deck with no posthole digging? Yes, it can be done.

Sometimes all you need is a simple, easy-to-build platform to complete an otherwise perfect backyard. The project shown here is an "island deck," detached from the house and requiring no ledger attachment and no deep digging to set posts.

That means it has the simplest of foundations; a set of precast concrete pier blocks that are simply set in place, making them far easier to work with than poured footings. The piers are cast to a standardized shape and size: 10 inches square and 10 inches high, with slots in the top to accommodate joists and posts. Because the pier blocks are not secured in the ground, the deck "floats." This allows for movement in response to settling and the freeze-thaw cycle of the soil. Floating pier decks meet most local codes—but check yours just to be sure.

This deck is also low enough to the ground that it won't require a handrail (unless your yard slopes severely off to one side).

TOOLS & MATERIALS

Preformed concrete pier blocks (25)
3" galvanized deck screws
Circular saw
Miter saw

Power drill and bits
Stain or sealer
Level
Chalk line

Work gloves
Eye and ear protection

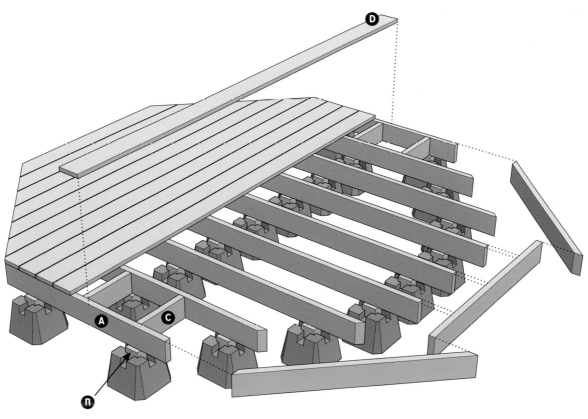

OVERALL SIZE: 10 × 10 FEET

CUTTING LIST

KEY	QUANTITY	SIZE	PART	MATERIAL
A	8	1½" × 5½" × 49¾"	Joist	PT pine
B	25	3½" × 3½" × (cut to fit)	Post	PT pine
C	6	1½" × 5½" × 13½"	Spreader	PT pine
D	22	1½" × 5½" × (cut to fit)	Decking	PT pine

How to Build a Floating Deck

Measure and mark the locations for the pier blocks. Position three rows of three blocks each. The rows for this deck were placed 46½ inches OC row to row, with 1½ inches OC between the pier blocks in each row. Check that each pier block is level, adding or removing dirt underneath to level it as necessary.

Set a 10-foot-long 2 × 6 joist on edge in the slots of the three pier blocks along one end of each row. Hold a carpenter's level along the top of the joist as a helper raises or lowers the lowest end of the joist. With the helper holding the joist level, measure any gaps between the bottom of the joist and the pier block sockets.

Cut 4 × 4 posts to match the gap measurements, and place the posts in the pier block sockets. Set the 2 × 6 joist on top of the posts, if any, and check for level again. Adjust as necessary. Only screw the joists down when the preliminary "box" for the frame is complete.

4

Cut 2 × 6 band joists for the ends of the floor joists. The band joists will be 49¾ inches long. Measure and mark the band joist so that it will extend equal lengths from both sides of where it is screwed to the floor joists. The first two opposite band joists complete the box.

5

Check diagonal measurements of the foundation center box. This must be square because the rest of the deck is built off the box. If the diagonal measurements are off at all, adjust the "box" until they match.

6

Complete the center of the deck frame by screwing the center joist into place, attaching it to the band joists on either end. Cut 4 × 4 posts as necessary to keep the joist level along its length and in relation to the two outside joists. Screw the joists to their 4 × 4 posts in toenail fashion.

7

Cut and position the outer floor joists in the octagon, leveling them in place as before. There should be a row of three piers and a row of two piers on each side of the center box.

8

Install the blocking to support the side piers. Once level, screw the outside joist to the 4 × 4 posts (if any) with the joist positioned so that the overhang on both sides is equal.

9

Drive 3" screws through the mitered ends to secure the band joists to one another. Use three screws per connection. Complete the outside frame by screwing diagonal band joists onto the mitered ends of the middle floor joists, and to the band joists.

Install the decking boards, allowing for overhang that will be trimmed at the end of construction. Begin laying the decking at one edge of the octagon so that the decking lays perpendicular to the floor joists.

Lay the rest of the decking boards by screwing them down to the joists, maintaining ⅛" spacing between boards. Screw down each decking board using two 3" deck screws per joist.

When all the decking boards have been screwed down, snap a chalk line along the edges over which the deck boards hang; use a circular saw equipped with a carbide blade to cut the deck board ends so that the decking is flush with the band joists. Stain, paint, or finish the deck as you prefer, including the rim joists. Add other built-on structures to suit your needs.

WALLS & FENCES

Crawling across a rolling field or guarding a suburban home, a fence or wall defines space and creates a backdrop for the enclosed landscape. Its materials, style, shape, and colors set a tone that may even tell you something about what you'll find on the other side.

Traditional picket fences conjure up images of cottage gardens and children playing. Post and rail fences often surround rustic landscapes or pastures; long expanses of a white board fence can make you believe there might be horses over the next hill. Privacy fences, such as board-and-stringer, or security fences, such as chain link, produce images of swimming pools sparkling in the sun.

Landscape walls can serve many purposes: They can define property boundaries, separate living areas within the yard, and screen off unpleasant views or utility spaces. Durable masonry walls, such as glass block, concrete block, stone, or stone veneer, can introduce new textures and patterns into your landscape, while living walls, like the framed trellis wall, can provide beautiful backdrops for your favorite vines or lush border gardens.

Using simple building techniques, the projects in this section offer a wide variety of choices for practical, visually appealing fences and walls. Properly constructed, the fences or walls you build should last decades with little maintenance.

Building with wood fence panels is a great time-saver and allows you to create a more elaborate fence than you may be able to build from scratch. Well-planned and designed fences can be important, pleasing parts of the landscape. Using two complementary fence styles can add visual interest.

WOOD PANEL FENCES

Prefabricated fence panels take much of the work out of putting up a fence, and (surprisingly) using them is often less expensive than building a board-and-stringer fence from scratch. They are best suited for relatively flat yards, but may be stepped down on slopes that aren't too steep.

Fence panels come in many styles, ranging from privacy to picket. Most tend to be built lighter than fences you'd make from scratch, with thinner wood for the stringers and siding. When shopping for panels, compare quality and heft of lumber and fasteners, as well as cost.

Purchase panels, gate hardware, and a gate (if you're not building one) before setting and trimming your posts. Determine also if panels can be trimmed or reproduced from scratch for short sections.

The most exacting task when building a panel fence involves insetting the panels between the posts. This requires that preset posts be precisely spaced and perfectly plumb.

In our inset panel sequence, we set one post at a time as the fence was built, so the attached panel position can determine the spacing, not the preset posts.

An alternative installation to setting panels between posts is to attach them to the post faces. Face-mounted panels are more forgiving of preset posts, since the attachment point of stringers doesn't need to be dead center on the posts.

Wood fence panels usually are constructed in either 6- or 8-foot lengths. Cedar and pressure-treated pine are the most common wood types used in making fence panels, although you may also find redwood in some areas. Generally, the cedar panels cost one-and-a-half to two times as much for similar styles in PT lumber.

When selecting wood fence panels, inspect every board in each panel carefully (and be sure to check both sides of the panel). These products are fairly susceptible to damage during shipping.

TOOLS & MATERIALS

Pressure-treated cedar or redwood 4 × 4 posts

Prefabricated fence panels

Corrosion-resistant fence brackets or panel hangers

Post caps

Corrosion-resistant deck screws (1", 3½")

Prefabricated gate & hardware

Wood blocks

Colored plastic

Tape measure

Plumb bob

Masking tape

Stakes and mason's string

Gravel

Clamshell digger or power auger

Hand tamp

Level

Lumber 2 × 4

Circular saw, hand saw, or reciprocating saw

Concrete

Drill

Line level

Clamps

Scrap lumber

Shovel

Hammer

Speed square

Eye and ear protection

Work gloves

Permanent marker

Hinges (3)

FENCE PANEL TYPES

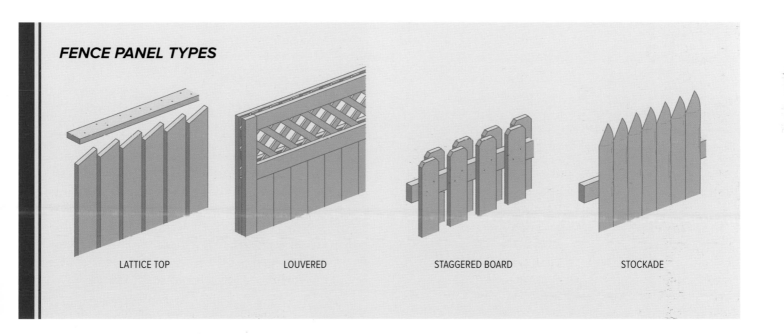

LATTICE TOP

LOUVERED

STAGGERED BOARD

STOCKADE

Tips for Installing Fence Panels

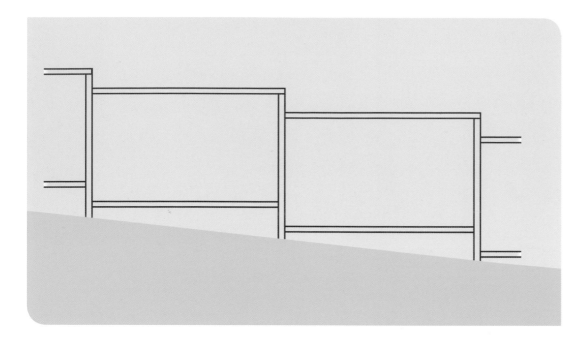

On a sloped lot, install the panels in a step pattern, trying to keep a consistent vertical drop between panels. It is difficult to cut most preassembled panels, so try to plan the layout so only full-width panels are used.

BEND TAB UP AFTER PANEL IS INSTALLED

Metal fence panel hangers make quick work of hanging panels and offer a slight amount of wiggle room if the panel is up to ½" narrower than the space between posts.

FLATTEN TAB WHEN INSTALLING HANGER

With some panel styles, the best tactic is to flatten the lower tab after attaching it to the post and then bend it up or down against the panel frame once the panel is in place.

How to Build a Wood-Panel Fence

Lay out the fenceline, and mark the posthole locations with colored plastic flags. Space the holes to fit the fence panels, adding the actual post width (3½" for 4 × 4 posts) plus ¼" for brackets to the panel length. *Tip: For stepped fences, measure the spacing along a level line, not along the slope.*

Dig the first posthole for a corner or end post using a clamshell digger or power auger. Add 6" of gravel into the hole, and tamp it flat. Set, plumb, and brace the first post with cross bracing.

Dig the second posthole using a 2 × 4 spacer to set the distance between posts (cut the spacer to the same length as the stringers on the preassembled fence panels).

Fill the first posthole with concrete or with tamped soil and gravel. Tamp the concrete with a 2 × 4 as you fill the hole. Let the concrete set.

Install the stringer brackets onto the first post using corrosion-resistant screws or nails. Shorter fences may have two brackets, while taller fences typically have three. *Note: The bottom of the fence siding boards should be at least 2" above the ground when the panel is installed.*

Set the first panel into the brackets. Shim underneath the free end of the panel with scrap lumber so that the stringers are level and the panel is properly aligned with the fenceline. Fasten the panel to the brackets with screws or nails.

Mark the second post for brackets. Set the post in its hole and hold it against the fence panel. Mark the positions of the panel stringers for installing the brackets. Remove the post and install the stringer brackets, as before.

Reset the second post, slipping the ends of the panel stringers into the brackets. Brace the post so it is plumb, making sure the panel remains level and is aligned with the fenceline. Fasten the brackets to the panel with screws or nails.

Anchor the second post in concrete. After the concrete sets, continue building the fence, following steps 5 to 8. *Option: You can wait to fill the remaining postholes with concrete until all of the panels are in place.*

Attach the post caps after trimming the posts to their finished height (use a level mason's line to mark all of the posts at the same height). Install the gate, if applicable.

VINYL PANEL FENCE

The best features of vinyl fencing are its resilience and durability. Vinyl fencing is made with a form of tough, weather-resistant, UV-protected PVC (polyvinyl chloride), a plastic compound that's found in numerous household products, from plumbing pipe to shower curtains. A vinyl fence never needs to be painted and should be guaranteed for decades not to rot, warp, or discolor. So if you like the styling of traditional wood fences, but minimal maintenance is a primary consideration, vinyl might just be your best option. Another good option is wood composite fencing, which comes in fewer styles than vinyl but is environmentally friendly and can replicate the look of wood fencing.

Installing most vinyl fencing is similar to building a wood-panel fence. With both materials, it's safest to set the posts as you go, using the infill panels to help you position the posts. Accurate post placement is critical with vinyl, because many types of panels cannot be trimmed if the posts are too close together. Squeezing the panel in can lead to buckling when the vinyl expands on hot days, while setting the posts too far apart results in unsightly gaps.

Given the limited workability of most vinyl panels, this fencing tends to work best on level or gently sloping ground. Keep in mind that installation of vinyl fences varies widely by manufacturer and fence style.

Vinyl fencing is available in a wide range of traditional designs, including picket, post and board, open rail, and solid panel. Color options are generally limited to various shades of white, tan, and gray.

Mason's string
Shovel
Clamshell digger or power auger
Circular saw
Drill
Tape measure
Hand maul
Line level

Post level
Clamps or duct tape
Concrete tools
Stakes
Lumber 2 × 4
Vinyl fence materials (with hardware, fasteners, and decorative accessories)
Pea gravel

Concrete
Pressure-treated 4 × 4 (for gate, if applicable)
PVC cement or screws (optional)
Work gloves
Post caps
Eye and ear protection

CUTTING PANELS

Cut panels for **short runs** on solid-panel fencing (if straight along the top) per manufacturer's recommendations. Often, the best way to cut plastic material is with a circular saw with the blade installed backwards.

How to Install a Vinyl Panel Fence

Lay out the first run of fence with stakes and mason's string. Position the string so it represents the outside or inside faces of the posts (you'll use layout strings to align the posts throughout the installation). Mark the center of the first post hole by measuring in from the string half the post width.

Dig the first posthole, following the manufacturer's requirements for diameter and depth (improper hole dimensions can void the warranty). Add 4" to 6" (or as directed) of pea gravel to the bottom of the hole and tamp it down using a 2 × 4 or 4 × 4 so it is flat and level.

Attach the fence panel brackets to the first post using the provided screws. Dry fit a fence panel into the brackets, then measure from the top of the post to the bottom edge of the panel. Add 2" (or as directed) to represent the distance between the fence and the ground; the total dimension is the posts' height above the ground.

Set up a post-top string to guide the post installation. Using the post height dimension, tie a mason's string between temporary 2 × 4 supports so the string is centered over the post locations. Use a line level to make sure the string is level. Measure from the string to the ground in several places to make sure the height is suitable along the entire fence run.

4

5

POST HEIGHT STRING

FENCE HINGE STRING

Determine the second post's location by fitting a fence panel into the brackets on the first post. Mark the ground at the free edge of the panel. Measure out from the mark half the post width to find the center of the post hole (accounting for any additional room needed for the panel brackets.)

Set the first post. Drop the post in its hole and align it with the fenceline string and height string. Install cross bracing to hold the post perfectly plumb. *Tip: Secure bracing boards to the post with spring-type clamps or duct tape. Fill the posthole with concrete and let it set completely.*

6

Complete the fence section. Dig the hole for the second post, add gravel, and tamp as before. Attach the panel brackets to the second post, set the post in place and check its height against the string line. Assemble the fence section with the provided screws. Confirm that the fence panel is level. Brace the second post in place (as shown) and anchor it with concrete. Repeat the same layout and construction steps to build the remaining fence sections. Add the post caps (inset). Depending on the product, caps may be installed with PVC cement or screws, or they may be fitted without fasteners. Add any additional decorative accessories, such as screw caps, to complete the installation.

PICKET FENCE

The quintessential symbol of American hominess, the classic picket fence remains a perennial favorite for more than its charm and good looks. It's also an effective boundary marker, creating a clear line of separation while appearing to be nothing more than a familiar decoration. This unique characteristic of a welcoming barrier makes the picket fence a good choice for enclosing an area in front of the house. It's also a popular option for separating a vegetable or flower garden from the surrounding landscape.

Building a custom picket fence from scratch is a great do-it-yourself project. The small scale and simple structure of the basic fence design make it easy to add your own creative details and personal touches. In this project, you'll see how to cut custom pickets and build a fence using standard lumber (plus an easy upgrade of adding decorative post caps). You can also buy precut pickets at home centers, lumberyards, and online retailers to save on the work of cutting your own.

Traditionally, a picket fence is about 3 to 4 feet tall (if taller than 4 feet, a picket fence starts to look like a barricade) with 1 × 3 or 1 × 4 pickets. Fence posts can be spaced anywhere up to 8 feet apart if you're using standard lightweight pickets. Depending on your preference, the posts can be visible design elements or they can hide behind a continuous line of pickets.

A low picket fence adds curb appeal and a cozy sense of enclosure to a front yard or entry area without blocking views to or from the house.

TOOLS & MATERIALS

Mason's string

Line level

Circular saw

Jigsaw

Drill

Power miter saw

Sander

2-foot level

Lumber (4 × 4, 2 × 4, 1 × 4)

Deck screws (3½", 2")

Finishing materials

Post caps (optional)

Hammer

Galvanized or stainless steel finish nails

Spacer

Speed square

Eye and ear protection

Clamps

Paintbrush

Tape measure

16d galvanized common nails

Wood sealant or primer

Work gloves

Pencil

Finish materials

CALCULATING PICKET SPACING

Determine the picket quantity and spacing. Cut a few pickets (steps 5 to 7) and experiment with different spacing to find the desired (approximate) gap between pickets. Calculate the precise gap dimension and number of pickets needed for each section using the formula shown in the example here.

Total space between posts: 92.5"

Unit size (picket width + approx. gap size): 3.5" + 1.75" = 5.25"

Number of pickets (post space ÷ unit size): 92.5" ÷ 5.25" = 17.62 (round down for slightly larger gaps, round up for slightly smaller gaps)

Total picket area (# of pickets × picket width): 17 × 3.5" = 59.5"

Remaining space for gaps (post space—total picket area): 92.5" − 59.5" = 33"

Individual gap size (total gap space ÷ [# of pickets + 1]): 33" ÷ 18 = 1.83"

To cut pickets with decorative custom shapes, create a cardboard or hardboard template with the desired shape. Trace the shape onto each picket and make the cuts. Use a jigsaw for curved cuts. Gang several cut pieces together for final shaping with a sander.

How to Build a Picket Fence

Install and trim the posts according to your plan. In this project, the pickets stand at 36" above grade, and the posts are 38" (without the post caps). Set the posts in concrete, and space them as desired—but no more than 96" apart on center.

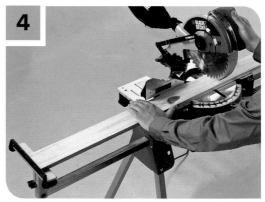

Mark the stringer positions onto the posts. Measure down from each post top and make marks at 8" and 28½" (or as desired for your design). These marks represent the top edges of the two stringer boards for each fence section.

Install the stringers. Measure between each pair of posts and cut the 2 × 4 stringers to fit. Drill angled pilot holes, and fasten the stringers to the posts with 3½" deck screws or 16d galvanized common nails; drive one fastener in the bottom and top edges of each stringer end.

Cut the pickets to length. To save time, set up a stop block with the distance from the block to blade equal to the picket length. Shape the picket ends as desired. For straight-cut designs, use a miter saw with a stop block on the right side of the blade (the first pass cuts through the picket and the block). If the shape is symmetrical, such as this 90-degree point, cut off one corner, and then flip the board over and make the second cut—no measuring or adjusting is needed. You can paint the pickets before or after installing them.

5

Set up a string line to guide the picket installation. Clamp a mason's string to two posts at the desired height for the tops of the pickets. *Note: To help prevent rot and to facilitate grass trimming, plan to install the pickets at least 2" above the ground.*

6

Install the pickets. Using a cleat spacer cut to the width of the picket gap, set each picket in place and drill even pairs of pilot holes into each stringer. Fasten the pickets with 2" deck screws. Check the first picket (and every few thereafter) for plumb with a level before piloting.

7

Add the post caps. Wood post caps (with or without metal cladding) offer an easy way to dress up plain posts while protecting the end grain from water. Install caps with galvanized or stainless steel finish nails, or as directed by the manufacturer. Apply the final finish coat or touch-ups to the entire fence.

A natural stone retaining wall blends into its surroundings immediately and only looks better with age. Building the wall with ashlar, or cut wall stone, is a much easier project than a wall built with round fieldstones or large boulders.

Rough-cut wall stones may be dry stacked (without mortar) to fashion retaining walls, garden walls, and other stonescape features. Dry-stack walls move and shift with the frost, and they drain well so they don't require deep footings and drain tiles.

In the project featured here, we use rough-split limestone blocks about 8 inches by about 4 inches thick and in varying lengths. Walls like this may be built up to 3 feet tall, but keep them shorter if you can, to be safe. Building multiple short walls is often a more effective way to manage a slope than to build one taller wall. Called terracing, this practice requires some planning. Ideally, the flat ground between walls will be approximately the same size.

A dry-laid natural stone retaining wall can be a very natural-looking structure compared to interlocking block retaining walls. One way to exploit the natural look is to plant some of your favorite stone-garden perennials in the joints as you build the wall. Usually one plant or a cluster of three will add interest to a wall without suffocating it in vegetation or compromising its stability. Avoid plants that get very large or develop thick, woody roots or stems that may affect the stability of the wall. A well-built retaining wall has a slight lean, called a batter, back into the slope. It has a solid base of compacted gravel, and the first course is set below grade for stability.

TOOLS & MATERIALS

Mason's string

Line level

Stakes

Hand maul

Torpedo level

Straight 2 × 4

Hand tamper

Compactable gravel

Ashlar wall stone

Landscape fabric

Caulk gun

Block and stone adhesive

Excavation tools

Coarse sand

Drainage gravel (1½" to 3" river rock is recommended)

Stone chisel

4-foot level

Tape measure

Hammer

Scissors

Work gloves

Eye and ear protection

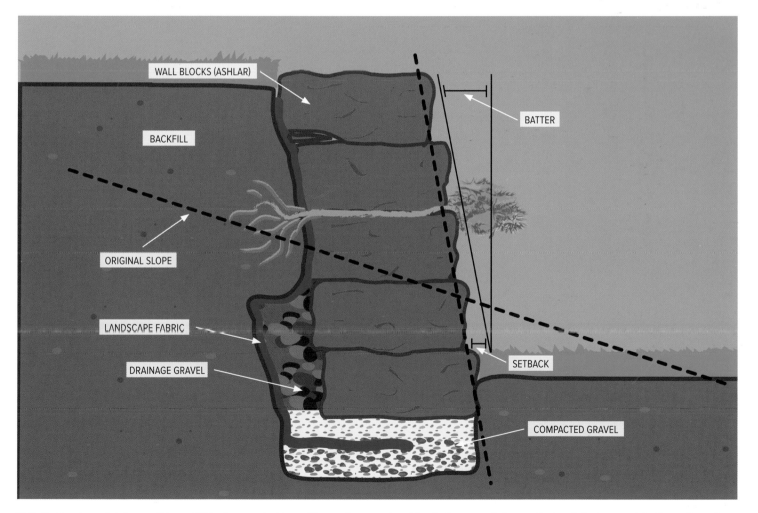

This single-row retaining wall has a ½" batter, created by setting each course of stone ½" back from the face of the course below. The base of the wall includes a compacted gravel subbase topped with sand to help level the first course of stones. Roots of plants sown into the wall crevices (an optional decorative embellishment) will eventually reach into the soil behind the wall.

How to Build a Stone Retaining Wall

Excavate the wall site. Dig a trench for the base of wall, making it 6" wider than the wall thickness. If necessary, dig into the slope, creating a backward angle that roughly follows the ½" batter the wall will have. If desired, dig returns back into the slope at the end(s) of the wall. Measure the depth of the trench against a level mason's string running parallel to the trench. The bottom of the trench should be level and 8" below grade for the main section of wall and any returns. If the trench becomes too shallow due to natural contours, step it down the height of one stone.

Complete the wall base by tamping the soil in the trench, and then adding a 3" layer of compactable gravel and tamping it flat and level. Cover the gravel with landscape fabric, draping the fabric back over the slope. Add a 1" layer of sand over the fabric in the trench area. Smooth and level the sand with a short 2 × 4 screed board, checking for level with a torpedo level set on the board.

Set the first course with heavy stones, laying long, square-ended stones at the corners first. Set up a level mason's string just in front of the top front edge of the course, letting the stones roughly guide the string placement. Add or remove sand beneath the stones as needed so they are nearly touching the string. Level the stones front to back with a torpedo level and side to side with a 4-foot level. If necessary, use a hand maul and stone chisel to chip off irregularities from the edges of the stones to improve their fit.

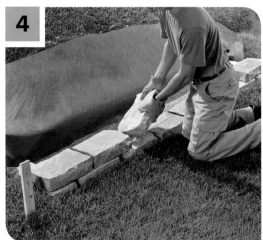

Begin the second course, starting with both ends of the wall face. Reset and level the mason's string at the height of the second course. Place the second-course stones back ½" from the front edges of the first-course stones, overlapping all joints of the first course to create a bond pattern.

5

Shim beneath stones as needed to level them or add stability, using stone shards and chips. Complete the second course over the main part of the wall. Complete the returns, as applicable, maintaining the offset joint pattern with the first course. You may need to dig into the slope to create a level base for the return stones. Add a layer of compacted gravel under each return stone before setting it. Complete the remaining courses up to the final (capstone) course.

6

Backfill behind the base of the wall with drainage rock (not compactable gravel). For a low wall like this, 6" to 10" of gravel is usually sufficient; taller walls may require more gravel and possibly a drainage pipe. Pack the gravel down with a 2 × 4 to help it settle.

7

Fold the landscape fabric over the gravel, and backfill over the fabric with soil. The fabric is used to prevent the soil from migrating into the gravel and out through the wall stones. Trim the fabric just behind the back of the wall, near the top.

8

Install the final course using long, flat cap stones. Glue the caps in place with block and stone adhesive. After the glue dries, add soil behind the wall to the desired elevation for planting.

Landscape block for freestanding walls is versatile and an easy material with which to build. You can use it to create low walls of almost any shape, plus columns, steps, and other features. Block manufacturers offer a variety of styles and textures, along with compatible specialty and accessory pieces for a well-integrated look.

Perhaps due to the huge popularity of interlocking concrete wall block, you can now find concrete landscape blocks made for a range of applications, including patio walls, freestanding columns, raised planters, and even outdoor kitchens. The blocks shown in this project require no mortar and are stacked up just like retaining wall units. Yet unlike retaining wall blocks, these freestanding units have at least two faceted faces, so the wall looks good on both sides. And they have flat bottoms, allowing them to be stacked straight up without a batter (the backward lean required for most retaining walls).

Solid concrete blocks for freestanding walls come in a range of styles and colors. Products that come in multiple sizes produce walls with a highly textured look that mimics natural stone, while walls made with uniform blocks have an appearance closer to weathered brick. Many block products can be used for both curved and straight walls, and most are compatible with cap units that give the wall an architecturally appropriate finish, as well as a great surface for sitting.

The wall in this project forms a uniform curve to follow the shape of a circular patio. It's built over a base of compacted gravel, but you could build the same wall right on top of a concrete patio slab. Keep in mind that freestanding walls like this are typically subject to height limits, which might range from 20 to 36 inches or perhaps higher. Walls with straight sections or gentle curves may need a supporting feature, such as a column or 90-degree turn or jog, to stabilize the wall.

Mason's string

Landscape marking paint

Excavation tools

Line level

Plate compactor or hand tamp

Rake

4-foot level

Caulk gun

Brickset or pitching chisel

Hand maul

Stone chisel

Wood stakes

Straight board

Compactable gravel

Concrete wall block and cap units

Concrete adhesive

Tape measure

Eye and ear protection

Circular saw with masonry blade (optional)

Heavy rope or garden hose

Wheelbarrow

Work gloves

Round over the cut edges of blocks to match the original texture. Using a stone chisel and mason's hammer or maul, carefully chip along the edges to achieve the desired look.

Cut blocks using a brickset or pitching chisel and a maul. First score along the cutting line all the way around the block, and then chisel at the line until the block splits. You can also cut a deep score line (on thick block) or cut completely through (on thin block) using a circular saw with a masonry blade.

How to Build a Freestanding Landscape Wall

1

Draw the rough outline of the wall onto the ground with a can of marking paint. First measure the wall blocks and/or align a few blocks in place as guides. To mark end columns, first measure the blocks and then use the marking paint to outline the footprint of the column.

2

Straight runs. Mark the outlines of the wall and/or excavation with stakes and mason's string. Position one string, then measure from it to position any remaining strings as needed. *Tip: Leave the stakes marking one of the wall faces in the ground; you'll use them later to align the wall block.*

3

Remove the sod and other plantings inside the excavation area. For a gravel base, the excavation should extend 6" beyond the wall on all sides. If you are building adjacent to a sandset patio with pavers, take care not to disturb the rigid paver edging. Alternatively, fully excavate the ground around the patio to compensate for the wall addition and install new edging around the perimeter.

4

Set up level lines to guide the excavation using stakes and mason's string. For curved walls, you may need more than one string. Level the string with a line level (make sure multiple strings are level with one another). Measure from the string to ground level (grade), and then add 12"—the total depth required for the excavation.

5

Use a story pole to measure the depth as you complete the excavation. To make a story pole, mark the finished depth of the excavation onto a straight board, and use it to measure against the string; this is easier than pulling out your tape measure for each measurement.

6

Tamp the soil in the trench with a rented plate compactor or a hand tamper. The bottom of the trench should be flat and level, with the soil thoroughly compacted. Take care not to disturb or damage adjacent structures.

7

Spread compactable gravel over the trench in an even 2"- to 3"-thick layer. Tamp the gravel thoroughly. Add the remaining gravel and tamp to create a 6"-thick layer after compaction. Check the gravel base with a level (or a level taped to a straight board) to make sure the surface is uniform and perfectly level. Add gravel to any low spots and tamp again.

8

Set the first course. If you're using more than one thickness of block, select only the thicker units for the first course. Lay out the blocks in the desired pattern along the layout line, butting the ends together for complete contact. If necessary, cut blocks to create the desired curve. Place a 4-foot level across the blocks to make sure they are level and flat across the tops.

Set the second course. Begin the course at the more visible end of the wall. Set the blocks in the desired pattern, making sure to overlap the block joints in the first course to create a bond pattern. Alternate different sizes of block, and check the entire course with a level. If necessary, cut a block for the end of the wall.

End each course with a piece no narrower than 6". If necessary, position a full unit at the end of the wall, then measure back and cut the second-to-last unit to fit the space. Glue small end pieces in place with concrete adhesive.

Complete the remaining courses, following the desired pattern. Be sure to maintain a bond with the course below by overlapping the joints in the lower course. For the top two courses, glue each block in place with concrete adhesive.

Install the cap blocks. Trapezoidal cap block may fit your wall's curve well enough without cuts (for gentle curves, try alternating the cap positions). If cuts are necessary, dry fit the pieces along the wall, and plan to cut every other block on both side edges for an even fit. Set all caps with concrete adhesive. Backfill along the wall to bury most or all of the first course.

How to Add Columns to a Freestanding Wall

1

Set the first course of each column after completing the first wall course (middle-of-wall columns are set along with each wall course). Use four full blocks for the first course, butting the column blocks against the end wall block. Check the column blocks for level.

2

Glue the second course and all subsequent courses in place with concrete adhesive or according to the manufacturer's specifications.

3

Cap the column with special cap units, or create your own caps with flagstone squares. Glue cap pieces in place with concrete adhesive or mortar in between them, following the manufacturer's instructions. *Tip: The hollow space in the column's center is ideal for running wiring for adding a light fixture on top of a cap.*

PLAY & ENTERTAINMENT PROJECTS

At the end of the day, your yard is really about play and entertainment. It is a space to run around in, or enjoy a breeze, or host a barbecue. And while the utility of a roomy shed or a sturdy fence cannot be denied, sometimes you just have to grab the fun ring.

In this chapter you will see only four projects executed in full detail. Two of them are play projects for kids, and two are outdoor cooking and entertaining projects. They are just the tip of the iceberg. Backyard fun and entertainment take a multitude of forms. These are four very popular and achievable DIY projects around which you can create many others. We encourage you to explore the wide universe of other possibilities.

Whether it is indoors or outdoors, a play structure should be absolutely safe. Pay attention to the instructions and advice about groundcover in and around them, and be responsible when it comes to supervising their usage. Projects that involve fire are always a concern of course. If you are building a fire pit or a pizza oven or anything else that involves burning, be sure to locate the project well away from permanent structures and low-hanging tree branches. Most municipalities have strict setback requirements for them and it is always a good idea to check with your local building department to find out what is recommended in your neighborhood.

BACKYARD FIRE PIT AND ROTISSERIE

This project can be very easy if you already have a fire pit—a matter of simply adding a purchased add-on rotisserie spit to an existing fire pit that you have in your yard. But we've also included complete instructions for building a great fire pit and safety pad you can build from scratch. You can adapt this project to whatever circumstances are found in your yard.

Rotisserie spits are available in many styles, from hand-cranked units to those with solar-powered motors to turn the spit. And they come in several different sizes, some appropriate to slow-cooking whole chickens or turkeys, others large enough to handle small goats or pigs. For most backyard fire pits, though, a 48- or 52-inch spit that just spans the fire pit itself is the best choice.

A fire pit with rotisserie can become a focal point and gathering spot for backyard entertaining and dining. The fire pit features here is constructed around a 36-inch corrugated metal liner, but you could also build it with a commercially available fire pit bowl or other enclosure available on any home center. We have surrounded the fire pit liner with cut limestone slabs, but this is just one option. Clay bricks, fire bricks, and retaining wall blocks are among other materials that could be used to build the surrounding walls.

Check with your local code for stipulations on the allowable size and location of your fire pit. For example, most municipalities have rules regarding how far a fire pit must be set back from fences or wooden structures in order to remain safe. Some localities may not allow outdoor burning at all.

Some pointers to consider when using your fire pit: 1) Make sure there are no bans in effect; 2) Evaluate wind conditions and avoid building a fire if winds are heavy and/or blowing toward your home; 3) Keep shovels, sand, water, and a fire extinguisher nearby; 4) Extinguish fire with water and never leave the fire pit unattended.

Wheelbarrow

Landscape paint

String and stakes

Spades

Metal pipe

Landscape edging

Level

Garden rake

Plate vibrator

Metal fireplace liner

Compactible gravel

Top-dressing rock or gravel

Wall stones

Eye and ear protection

Work gloves

Cross Section: Fire Pit

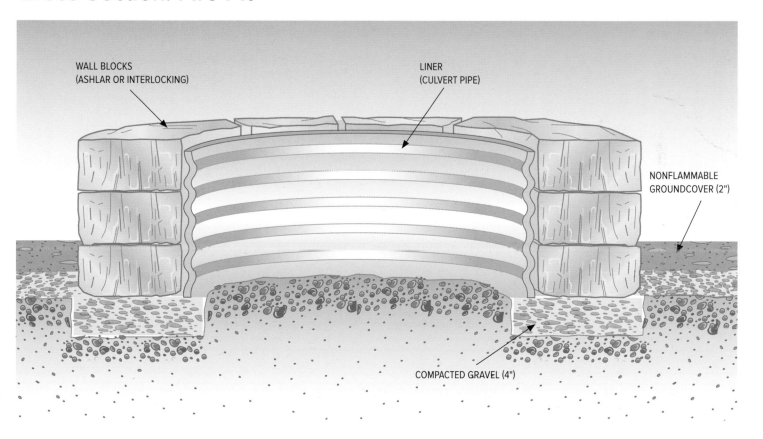

WALL BLOCKS
(ASHLAR OR INTERLOCKING)

LINER
(CULVERT PIPE)

NONFLAMMABLE
GROUNDCOVER (2")

COMPACTED GRAVEL (4")

How to Build a Fire Pit and Rotisserie

Outline the location for your fire pit and the fire pit safety area by drawing concentric circles with landscape paint, using a string and pole for guidance. Remove a 4"-deep layer of sod and dirt in the fire pit and safety areas (the depth of excavation depends on what materials you're installing in the safety zone).

Dig a 4"-deep trench for the perimeter stones that will ring the liner pit.

Place your metal fire ring so it is level on the gravel layer and centered around the center pipe.

Fill the trench for the perimeter stones with compactable gravel and tamp thoroughly. Then scatter gravel to within 2½" of the paver edging throughout the project area. It is not necessary to tamp this layer at this time.

5

Arrange the first course of wall blocks around the fire ring. Keep gaps even and check with a level, adding or removing gravel as needed.

6

Install the second course of wall block, taking care to evenly stagger the vertical joints on the first and second courses. Add the remaining courses to the desired height. Compact the gravel in the seating/safety area using a rental plate vibrator.

7

Place and compact a layer of top-dressing rock in the seating/safety area to complete the fire pit.

How to Add a Rotisserie to the Fire Pit

Choose a location for the two upright support posts. The span between the posts depends on the kit you buy, but typically you would seek to place the uprights as close to the inside edges of the fire pit as you can. These posts will get very hot, and it's a good ideal to keep them inside within the boundaries of the fire pit. With a mallet, drive the blunt ends of the posts down into the ground, taking care to keep them perfectly plumb.

Insert the motor head bracket onto the larger-diameter support post. The head should be installed so the thumb latch on top of the motor head bracket faces upward. To adjust the height up or down, squeeze the thumb latch, slide the bracket to the desired height, and release the thumb latch to fix the motor in place.

To install the motor, locate the motor support slots located on the outside of the motor support bracket. Insert the bottom of the motor mounting tabs into the top of the slots and push the motor down into position. Take care not to install the motor upside down.

Begin assembly of the handle unit by sliding the outboard support clamp onto the smaller support post so the U-shaped cutout faces upward. Adjusting height is done by squeezing the tabs on the clap and sliding the clamp up or down on the support post.

5

Slide the thumbscrew bushing onto the threaded end of the spit rod rust past the threads. Screw down the thumbscrew tightly.

6

Place the looped end of the counterbalance over the threads on the spit rod and against the lock nut on the bushing.

7

Thread the handle onto the spit rod. Insert the spit rod into the motor assembly on the opposite post. Tighten the bushing thumbscrew down to lock it in place.

8

Even weight distribution is critical in rotisserie cooking, and here is where the counterbalance comes in. Once a food item is secured in the prongs on the spit rod, find the heaviest side of the food, then manually turn the rod until this heaviest portion is facing up. Allow the counterweight to point straight downward, and secure the handle to hold it in place. This will allow the spit to be relatively balanced so the motor can function smoothly. As the food item cooks and shrinks, you can expect to readjust the counterweight several times.

If you truly want the best pizza in town, make it at home in your own wood-fired oven. This is not an exaggeration. You really can't beat homemade pizza cooked in a wood-fired oven, and you can't begin to get the same flavors in your regular oven.

A pizza oven isn't just the preferred cooker for pizza—it's also the ultimate centerpiece for outdoor entertaining. And it cooks a lot more than pizza. If you want to spellbind your guests with meat instead, grill a *bistecca Fiorentina* on a grate right over the coals, or char some red peppers next to the fire. The even heat radiating from the brick on all sides makes the oven great for baking, too.

The brick oven in this project is based on a traditional barrel-dome design and is the easiest type of oven to build. The brick is a high-temperature firebrick that is commonly available at home centers and masonry suppliers. Be sure to use medium-duty firebrick and refractory mortar, as standard types of brick and mortar can't handle the heat of the cooking fire. Before using the oven for cooking, you must heat cure it by burning progressively hotter fires over a period of five days. This prevents cracking of the masonry when using the oven at high cooking temperatures.

The floor and dome of the oven must be built over a structural base of masonry or other noncombustible material. The base structure shown here consists of concrete block walls topped with 2-inch-thick concrete pavers. The block walls need a solid foundation that resists ground movement. The ideal foundation is an existing concrete slab, such as a concrete patio. If you must build a new foundation, consult the local building department to learn about structural requirements for your project. For the horizontal structure on top of the walls, it's easiest to use a reinforced precast concrete slab from a local supplier. If this is difficult to find or prohibitively expensive, constructing the horizontal top slab from separate pavers works well.

Constructing the oven requires some basic masonry techniques, including cutting brick and block, mixing and applying mortar, and finishing mortar joints. Because masonry materials vary in size, the dimensions of any part of your oven may differ from those given here, and you may need to modify your brick form based on the actual dimensions of your firebrick.

TOOLS & MATERIALS

- 2 × 4 lumber for template
- Framing square
- Mortar mixing tub
- Bricklayer's trowel
- 4-foot level
- Rubber mallet
- Jointing tool
- Square-end trowel
- Circular saw with wood blades and masonry blade
- Jigsaw
- Wooden yardstick or straight board to use as trammel
- Finish nail

- Drill-driver and drill bits
- Brickset chisel
- Maul
- Stiff-bristle brush
- Infrared thermometer
- Standard concrete blocks, 8" × 8" × 16" (15)
- Combination corner concrete blocks, 8" × 8" × 16" (15)
- Half-block concrete blocks, 8" × 8" × 8" (5)
- Type S mortar
- One-coat stucco or surface-bonding cement mix

- Eye and ear protection
- Work gloves
- 2" × 24" concrete paver slabs (4)
- 1½" × 16" steel angle iron (2)
- ¾" × 4' × 8' plywood
- ⅛" × 4' × 8' hardboard
- 1½" coarse-thread drywall screws
- Duct tape
- 9" × 4½" × 2½" medium-duty firebricks (150)
- Refractory mortar
- 3" galvanized chimney flue with cap (I.D.)

CUTTING LIST

KEY	QUANTITY	SIZE	PART	MATERIAL
A	1	¾" × 28¼" × 38"	Form base	¾" plywood
B	3	¾" × 28¼" × 13 ⅜"	Form rib	¾" plywood
C	1	⅛" × 38" × 89½"	Form top	⅛" hardboard

BRICK FORM

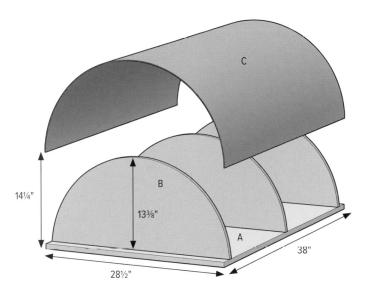

OVEN FLOOR PATTERN

FRONT VIEW

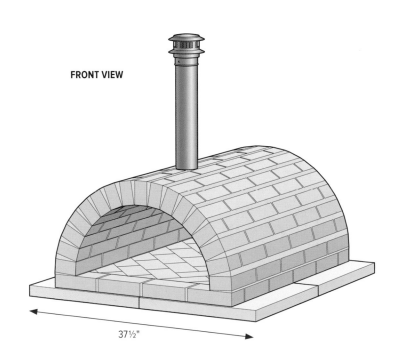

REAR VIEW

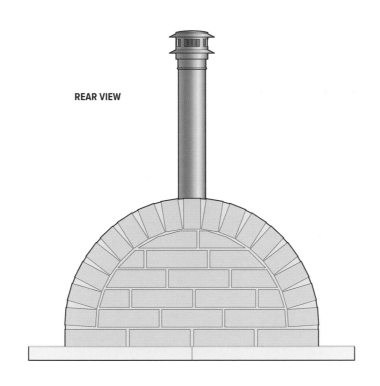

PIZZA OVEN—OPTIONAL BASE

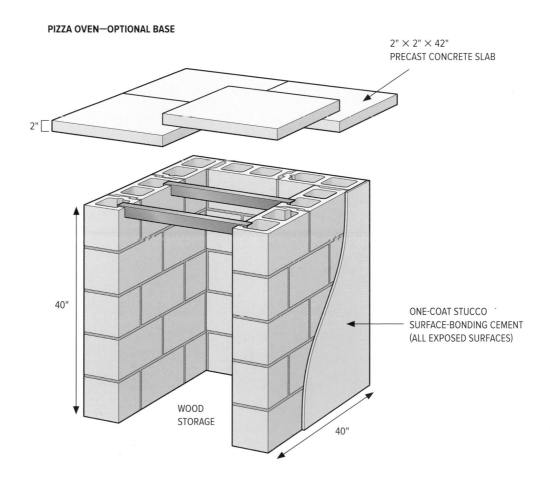

2" × 2" × 42"
PRECAST CONCRETE SLAB

2"

40"

ONE-COAT STUCCO
SURFACE-BONDING CEMENT
(ALL EXPOSED SURFACES)

WOOD
STORAGE

40"

How to Build the Optional Base

Set the 40" square base for your pizza oven. If you are building your oven on an existing slab, this is simply a matter of outlining the foundation on the slab. But in our example, the oven was being built in the yard. We built a gravel-lined trench according to local building code specifications. Always check with your local building code office for recommendations on what type of foundation is required. Build a 2 × 4 guide form to help establish the first course of blocks, and measure diagonally to make sure the template is square. If the measurements are equal, the outline is square. If not, make small adjustments to square up the template.

Set the first course of concrete blocks in type S mortar. Start one of the side walls with a half block at the front of the base. Complete the course down the first wall, across the rear wall, and up the other side wall, finishing with a corner block. Check the blocks in the first course with a 4' level. All of the blocks should be level with one another in all directions. Use a rubber mallet to tap the blocks into alignment. Making the first row level helps ensure that subsequent courses will be level. Once the first course has set, you can remove the guide form.

Set the next courses of blocks, starting with a corner block at the front of the first wall to create a running-bond brick pattern in which the vertical seams are offset. Tool the mortar joints with a jointing tool as you go. Repeat the process to complete the three remaining courses, for a total of five. Tool the joints after every two rows are laid. Let the mortar cure as directed by the manufacturer before moving on to the next step. This will require at least an overnight curing period.

Finish the interior and exterior sides of the block walls with one-coat stucco or surface-bonding cement, using a square-end trowel and following the manufacturer's directions. Let the stucco cure as directed.

You will install 16" angle irons across the top row of the foundation to support the front of the concrete pavers and the joint between the first and second row of pavers. Use a circular saw with a masonry blade to cut a kerf into the top of the blocks to fit the vertical flange on the angle irons. Set the angle irons in place, then apply a ½"-thick layer of mortar to the tops of the base walls. Set the concrete pavers onto the mortar, and make sure they are level from side to side and front to back. Tool the mortar beneath the edges of the pavers and allow to cure fully—at least overnight.

How to Build a Brick Pizza Oven

Cut the base of the brick form to size from ¾" plywood, using a circular saw. Cut the arching base top to size from ⅛" hardboard.

Draw a semicircle for one of the base ribs using a homemade trammel. Make the trammel by drilling a small hole for a finish nail about 1" from the end of a wooden yardstick or a thin, straight board. Drill another hole 13 ⅜" away from the first hole. Drive a finish nail through the first hole and into the ¾" plywood, very close to one of the factory (uncut) edges of the panel. Position a pencil in the other hole of the trammel and rotate the trammel to draw the semicircle on the plywood.

Cut out the first rib with a jigsaw. Using the first rib as a template, trace the outlines for two more ribs, then cut them out. Mark three layout lines for the ribs onto both faces of the plywood form base. Locate the two outside lines 3" from each end of the base, and center the third rib in the middle of the base, using a framing square to mark the lines. Center each rib over a line and fasten it to the base with 1½" drywall screws driven through the base and into the edge grain of the rib.

4

Attach the hardboard form top by fastening it to the side edges of the plywood base, using 1½" drywall screws driven every 4" to 5". The smooth side of the hardboard should face out. Bend the hardboard over the ribs, screwing it down to the ribs as you go. Fasten the hardboard along the other base side, as with the first side.

5

Begin building the oven by centering the brick form on top of the concrete pavers. Lay a ⅜"-thick bed of refractory mortar and set the first course of firebrick along the base of the form. In our design, it was possible to use full bricks all the way around the form; however, if your bricks are a slightly different size, you may need to cut some of the bricks. If so, it's best to do this on the back corners, where they will be less visible. Let the mortar cure overnight, then remove the brick form.

6

Dry-lay the firebricks for the oven floor, following the herringbone pattern shown on page 84, or using a different diagonal pattern, if you desire. Cut the bricks to fit along the edges, using a circular saw with masonry blade to score the bricks, then breaking them with a brickset chisel and hammer. Fill in the entire floor, then remove the bricks one at a time and set them aside in the same pattern.

7

Cover the floor area with an even, ⅜"-thick layer of refractory mortar. Set the floor bricks into the mortar in your established pattern. Do not apply mortar between the bricks. Use the 4' level to ensure all the floor bricks are level with one another and with the perimeter bricks. The floor area must be level and smooth, with no raised edges between bricks. Let the mortar cure, at least overnight.

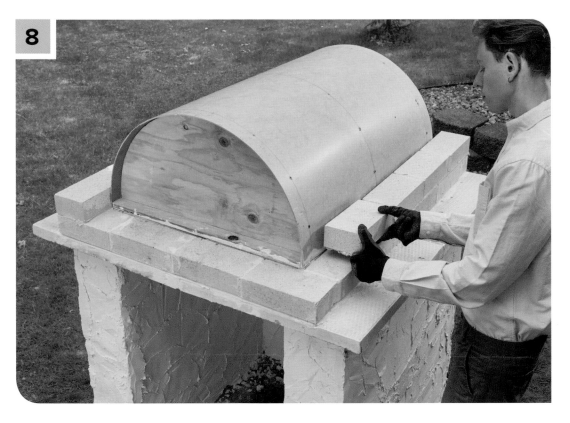

8

Place the brick form on top of the oven floor so it is centered side to side and front to back. Begin building the oven dome by setting one course of firebrick along the two sides of the oven, staggering the mortar joints with the courses below in an offset, running-bond pattern. At the ends of rows, you will need to cut bricks to size with a circular saw and masonry blade. Check your work with a level as you go.

Complete five more courses on each side of the dome, following the same running-bond pattern. Because half blocks are not supported by the interior form, you will need to cut small braces to hold the half blocks in place as the dome gets higher. Because of the arching pattern, the joints between bricks will be much wider on the outside of the bricks, while on the inside, the joints will nearly touch. Gradually, you will arch over the top of the form, meeting in the center. As you near the top of the arch, test-fit bricks periodically to ensure that you will meet in the center with full bricks. If you need to begin adjusting the thickness of the mortar lines to ensure a uniform fit, now is the time to do it.

9

Lay the brick for the last two courses to complete the dome. Start with a half brick at the front, then leave a 3½" space before resuming the running-bond pattern for the remainder of both courses. The space is an opening for the chimney.

Install the metal chimney flue so it is centered over the hole in the dome and perfectly plumb. Pack refractory mortar around the chimney to hold it in place. Let the mortar for the chimney and dome cure for two days or as directed by the mortar manufacturer.

Remove the brick form. This may require prying and cutting away pieces of the form in order to extract it. Begin by knocking loose the ribs, then pry away the hardboard arch. Finish by prying out the base of the form. Now, enclose the rear of the oven with courses of firebrick. You will need to cut some small angled pieces of brick at the edges. Let the mortar cure for two days.

13

Clean the entire oven inside and out with water and a stiff-bristle brush to remove all loose mortar and other debris. If mortar is resisting removal, use a diluted muriatic acid solution, following the manufacturer's directions. Let the mortar cure for seven days. The oven does not need to stay dry for this period.

14

Heat-cure the oven by burning gradually larger fires on the center of the oven floor for a period of five days following the schedule shown below. Monitor the temperature during each firing using an infrared thermometer. Aim the thermometer at the center of the dome interior, directly above the fire.

FIRING SCHEDULE

Burn the fire for at least 6 hours each day, maintaining the correct temperature for that day, as shown in this schedule. Use only hardwood firewood, not sappy wood (such as pine) or charcoal briquettes. Keep the fires small, just large enough to maintain the target temperature. The flames should not reach the oven dome. Do not exceed the target temperature. After five days of firing, you can begin burning fires hot enough to cook pizza, approximately 700°F to 800°F, as measured on the oven floor.

DAY	TARGET TEMPERATURE
1	300°F
2	350°F
3	400°F
4	450°F
5	500°F

Precut playground packages contain everything you need except tools. A homeowner with basic skills can put together a play area like this in one or two weekends.

If you want to design and build a backyard playground that meets your needs, but you don't want to start from scratch, a good option is to buy a precut playground kit. Most home centers and a number of internet suppliers sell do-it-yourself playground packages containing parts and hardware to make a complete play area. Some of the kits include all of the wood, while others include a list of lumber that you must buy with the set. Dozens of different designs are available, from a basic swingset and slide to elaborate, multilevel play areas with numerous extra features. Most manufacturers design their systems so that optional features can be easily added on.

Most playground systems are designed to be installed with poured concrete footings, but in some cases you may be able to get by with simply anchoring the posts. If you choose not to pour footings, it's even more important for the ground underneath the tower and swingset to be very level. To level and smooth the playground area and to stop grass and weeds from growing through it, cut out the sod in the play area, or at least in the area where the structures go, before you begin building.

NOTE: The instructions in the following project are intended as a general guide for installing a playground kit that includes precut lumber. The type of playground you purchase may use different materials and techniques than shown here.

TOOLS & MATERIALS

Framing square

Carpenter's level

Socket wrench

Adjustable wrench

Drill-driver

Sawhorses

Shovels

Posthole digger

Stakes

Mason's string

Line level

Circular saw

Clamps

Ladder

Spacers

Screwdriver

Lag screws

Anchor screws

Playset kit

Eye and ear protection

Work gloves

Lumber 02 × 6 or 2 × 8

Brackets

Bolts

1½", 2½" deck screws

Tape measure

Swing hangers

1½" panhead screws

Landscape fabric

Mulch

Screw-in anchors

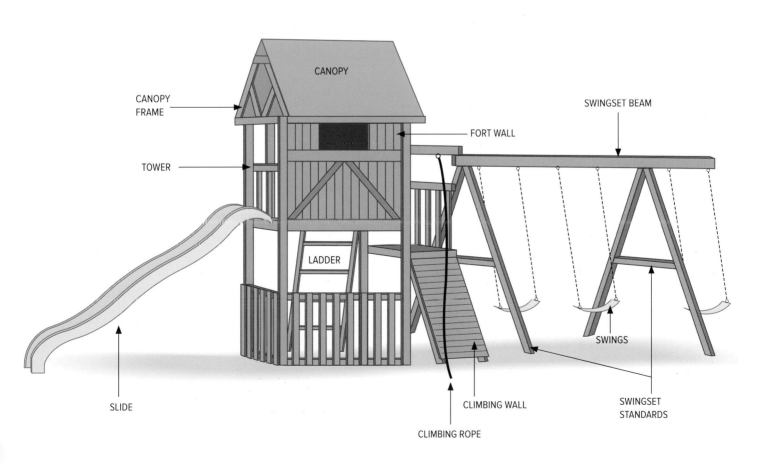

How to Install a Playground Kit

Prepare the installation area. Use strings and stakes to outline the area and then cut out the sod in the play area. Level the ground. Where possible, level the ground using the lowest spot as a starting point and excavating high areas to that point. Add landscape fabric. Begin assembling a tower. Towers are the principal structural elements in any playground kit. They support slides and other accessories. Generally, they are composed of fairly simple frames and beams. For the kit shown here, assemble the framework of the tower one side at a time, and then join the sides together on top of flat pieces of 2 × 6 or 2 × 8. Use the drilling template included in the kit as a guide for driving countersunk screws. Raise the tower.

Screw the brackets to the tower frame corners, making sure that the bolt hole on the long side of the bracket lines up with the centers of the 2 × 4s behind it. Using the large holes in the brackets as guides, drill holes for the bolts. To avoid splintering the back sides, stop drilling as soon as the bit starts to poke through the back, then finish drilling from the other side. Check to make sure everything is still square, and then install and tighten the bolts.

Install the center joists that connect the platform frames, fastening them with countersunk 2½" deck screws. Make certain all screw heads are fully seated beneath the wood surface.

4

Install the deckboards with 1½" deck screws driven into countersunk pilot holes, starting with the two outside pieces. Try to make sure the ends of the deck boards are aligned during installation—clamping a stop block or spacer block to the deck-board support will help align your work pieces. The drainage gaps between the deck boards must be less than ¼".

5

Extend the tower walls to the full height with additional 2 × 4 pieces. Use the drill guide or template (if provided with your kit) to ensure regular alignment of all screws.

6

Install the outer framework of 2 × 4s to support the roof of the playground structure, using corner brackets provided by the kit manufacturer.

Add additional framing to strengthen the sides of the tower. The framing on the right will help support the swingset and the climbing bar and climbing wall; the 2 × 4s on the left are used to support the slide.

Install the bottom railings and the top back and side railings for the tower structure. Clamp a straight piece of wood on top of (or underneath) the railing at the 1" point to create the setback and to make installation easier. Cut spacers to make the gap even, but check the gap before screwing in the last few boards, just in case, and adjust if necessary.

Attach railings, siding, and trim. Install the front railing first, using a ³⁄₁₆" spacer. Then, add the trim pieces. This step is easier if you tilt the structure backwards to the ground—but don't try this without a helper.

Install the rest of the roof frame. Use clamps to hold pieces in position before attaching them. Check the center vertical pieces with a carpenter's level to make sure they are plumb.

11

12

Begin building the swingset. The swing structure shown here is supported by a pair of angled posts in an A-frame configuration on the end opposite from the tower, and a single angled leg on the tower end. Fasten the three legs of the swingset together (they are made with doubled 2 × 4s), and then bolt on the triangular bracket for each leg. Construct the assembly by bolting the triangular brackets together and then screwing on the crosspiece. Add the small brackets to the inside of the crosspiece, with the short legs against the crosspiece (inset). Trim the leg bottoms so they lie flat on the ground.

Join the beams and legs. Screw the 2 × 6 beam pieces to the brackets, making sure the legs are exactly parallel and square to the beam. Drill the ⅜" holes for the bolts using the brackets as a guide. Then screw the second layer of 2 × 6s to the first with 2½" screws.

13

SWING
HANGER

Attach the swing hardware. Turn the swing assembly over and place it on sawhorses. Drill guide holes and fasten the sides together with bolts. Drill guide holes for the swing hangers and lag screws and install them so that the moving hanger swings perpendicular to the beam.

14

Add the swingset to the tower. Lift the swingset into place and fasten it to the tower with a bolt through the swing beam and a 2 × 4 crosspiece near the base fastened with metal angles and bolts.

15

Install the climbing wall. Attach the climbing wall supports to the tower frame with the provided brackets. The ends of the supports are angle-cut at the top and the bottom. Attach the top and bottom crossboards to the outer supports and then center the middle support board and attach it by driving deck screws through the crossboards and into the support.

16

Add the remaining crossboards in the climbing wall, working down from the top and making sure the boards are fitted tightly together.

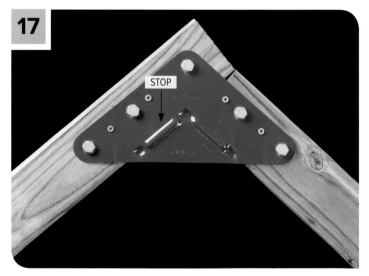

17

Start building the climbing bar assembly. The climbing bars function as a ladder that is mounted to the tower on the side opposite the climbing wall. Assemble the climbing bar standards with four triangular metal brackets included with the kit. The stops on the sides of the brackets that contact the standard will set the correct angle for the standards if the boards are tight against the stops.

18

Attach the climbing bars to the standards, making sure the standards are parallel and oriented correctly. Use 1½" panhead screws to attach the bars at 12" intervals on the bottom leg and at 10¾" intervals along the top.

19

Connect the climbing bar to the tower. First, dig holes into the play surface at the correct locations for the legs of the climbing bar standards. Set the legs into the 2"-deep holes, and then fasten the top ends of the standards to the tower with brackets and lag screws.

20

Anchor all the sides of the swingset, along with the climbing bar and climbing wall, using screw-in anchors. If the anchors don't work properly in your soil type, dig a 2-foot-deep post hole, fill it with concrete, and set the anchor in that. Bolt the anchor to the structure with ⅜" × 1½" lag screws.

21

Attach the slide. First, position the slide and then attach it to the tower at the top with fasteners. Then, bolt the side at the base to a screw-in anchor. Add other accessories as you choose.

SWINGSET

Swingsets are the most popular and common playground feature, and for good reason. There is something eternally pleasing about the simple back-and-forth rhythm of a swing in motion. It's relaxing, enjoyable, and entertaining (even for adult kids). That's why a backyard swingset is an absolute must-have for any home with children.

Stability is priority number one when it comes to building a swingset. The joints must be secured for safety and longevity—something that is achieved in this structure using special A-frame brackets, and 2 × 6 cross braces. To ensure absolute stability, each leg should be anchored in place to solid ground, not just set on top of loose infill.

Swings are virtually a requirement in any playset. This swingset is bolted to a DIY playset, but it can easily be modified into a freestanding swinging structure.

TOOLS & MATERIALS

Pencil

Circular saw

Protractor

Power miter saw

Drill-driver

Spade bit

Sawhorses

Clamps

Stepladder

Eye and ear protection

Work gloves

(8) ⅜" × 5" carriage bolts, nuts, washers

(2) ⅜" × 6" carriage bolts, nuts, washers

(2) Swingworks A-frame brackets (see Resources, page 143)

Swing seats, chains, and hardware

CUTTING LIST

KEY	QUANTITY	SIZE	MATERIAL	
A	4	3½" × 3½" × 104"	PT pine	
B	1	3½' × 5½' × 8'	PT pine	
C	2	1½' × 5½' × 6'	PT pine	

How to Build a Swingset

Mark the posts for cutting. If you are using A-frame brackets (strongly recommended), purchase the hardware beforehand and mark the posts using the A-frame bracket as a guide. If you are not using brackets, use a protractor or a speed square as a gauge to mark the tops of the posts at around 65 degrees so they will meet to form a stable A-shaped structure with sufficient leg spread.

Cut the long angles on each post with a circular saw, then square off the top edge with a power miter saw or circular saw.

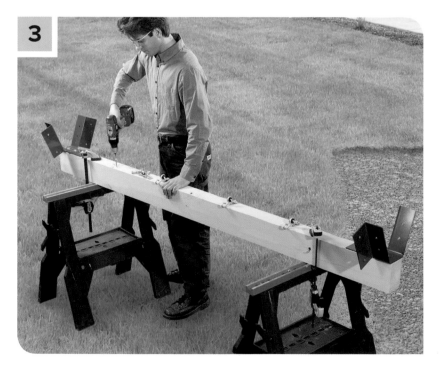

Bolt the A-frame brackets onto the 4 × 6, and then predrill the holes for the eye bolts that hold the swing. Use a long spade bit for the eye bolt holes.

Assemble the legs. Lay the 4 × 4 legs for one side on a flat area, set the 4 × 6 on top of them, and then bolt the legs to the brackets. Use the fasteners recommended by the hardware manufacturer. You'll need a helper to hold the 4 × 6 steady.

5

Attach the second leg. Use a stepladder or helpers to hold the 4 × 4s steady and in place as you finish bolting into the brackets.

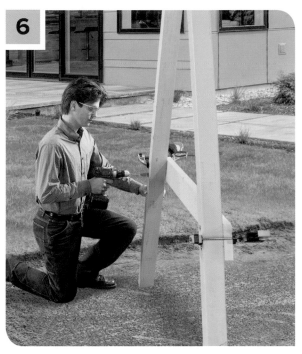

6

Clamp the 2 × 6 ties in position. Drill the bolt holes, and then counterbore the holes on the inside. Bolt the 2 × 6 on with 5" carriage bolts.

7

Anchor the swingset. Tack the swingset structure in place against the platform of the adjoining playset. Using a long drill bit, drill through each 4 × 4 leg and bolt the swing to the platform.

8

Hang the swings using the mounting hardware and chains or rope supplied or recommended by the manufacturer. Test to make sure the ground clearance is adequate and adjust as necessary.

SHEDS & STRUCTURES

Decks and patios and pathways are wonderful additions to any outdoor environment. But at some point you'll want to create a building. It is every DIYer's dream. Short of constructing your own home or your cabin in the woods, your yard offers many opportunities to create an outbuilding. It could be a shed or an arbor or pergola, or perhaps simply a firewood shelter. But creating a permanent structure in your yard is a meaningful step forward in your DIY experience, and you'll enjoy every moment you spend in your new outbuilding.

A shed is a perfect project for the ambitious DIYer. The construction demands are less rigorous than those of a more complex structure, such as a house. However, even a small shed should be built with sturdy structural elements to withstand time, insects, and the elements. That's why the lumber most commonly used in sheds is pressure-treated softwoods or a naturally resistant wood, such as cedar. Pressure-treated lumber is normally your cheapest option for most outdoor building projects, but it is also the least attractive. That makes it best for foundation and framing pieces that will be clad in another material, or painted. It's a good choice for sheds in which interior walls will be left unfinished and much of the wood will be left exposed to the elements and variations in temperature.

In most cases, a small outbuilding or permanent yard structure does not require a building permit. There are covenants that limit how much of your yard may be occupied by permanent structures, but in most municipalities if your shed or arbor has a footprint of less than 120 square feet, you do not need a permit to build it. Do make sure you comply with local setback requirements, which generally mandate that your shed or structure should be at least 5 feet away from your property line.

ANATOMY OF A SHED

Shown as a cutaway, this shed illustrates many of the standard building components and how they fit together. It can also help you understand the major construction stages—each project in this book includes a specific construction sequence, but most follow the standard stages in some form:

1. Foundation—including preparing the site and adding a drainage bed;

2. Framing—the floor is first, followed by the walls, then the roof;

3. Roofing—adding sheathing, building paper, and roofing material;

4. Exterior finishes—including siding, trim, doors, and windows.

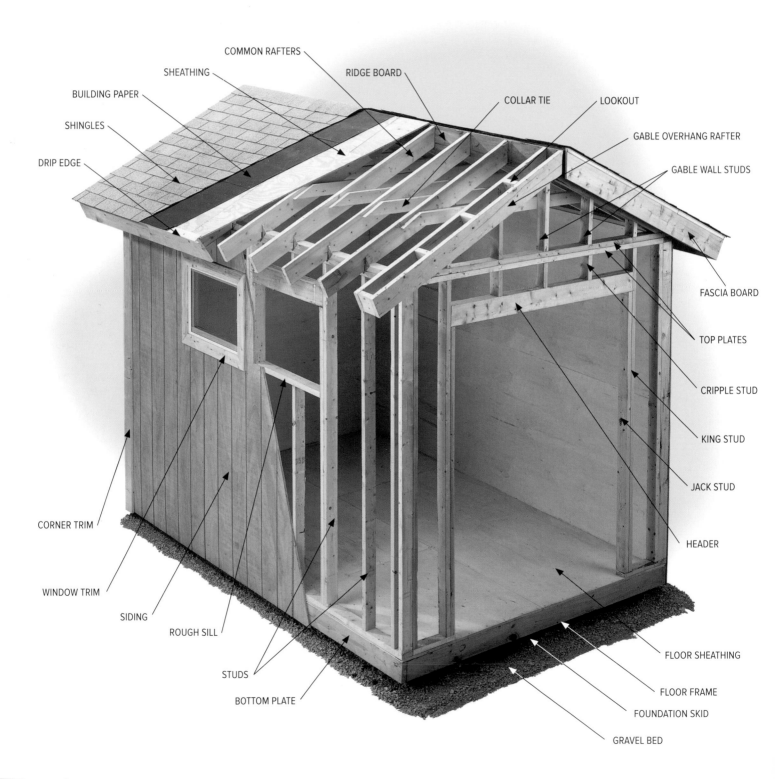

CONCRETE SLAB FOUNDATION

The slab foundation commonly used for larger sheds (and garages) is called a slab-on-grade foundation. This combines a 3½- to 4-inch-thick concrete floor slab with an 8- to 12-inch-thick perimeter footing that provides extra support for the walls of the building. The whole foundation can be poured at one time using a simple wood form.

Because they sit above ground, slab-on-grade foundations are susceptible to frost heave. Specific design requirements also vary by locality, so check with the local building department regarding the depth of the slab, the metal reinforcement required, the type and amount of gravel required for the subbase, and whether plastic or another type of moisture barrier is needed under the slab.

The slab shown below has a 3½-inch-thick interior with an 8-inch-wide × 8-inch-deep footing perimeter. There is a 4-inch layer of compacted gravel underneath the slab and perimeter, and the concrete is reinforced internally with a layer of welded wire mesh (WWM), as well as number 4 rebar in the perimeter. After the concrete is poured and finished, 8-inch galvanized J-bolts are set into the slab along the edges. These are used to anchor the shed wall framing to the slab.

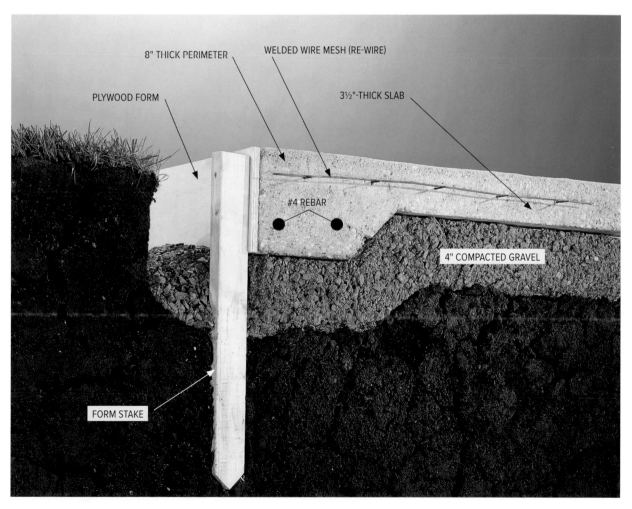

Cross section of a Concrete Slab Foundation

GARBAGE & RECYCLING SHED

Trash cans and recycling containers are essential fixtures for any house. If you don't have garage space (or don't want the smells and potential leaks in the garage), you're forced to put these less-than-attractive containers on the outside of your house. No matter where you place them, they don't improve the look of the house or the yard. To make matters worse, area wildlife and even neighborhood dogs find trash cans an irresistible lure. The answer to all those concerns is, of course, this simple, useful, and handsome shed.

This particular shed has been designed with no floor or built foundation. The structure is basically a shell that rests on a U-shaped base of pressure-treated 4 × 4s and a façade fabricated from pressure-treated 2 × 4s and durable T1-11 siding. The construction is still rugged enough to protect and secure garbage and recycling wherever you choose to put it—even if it is exposed to the elements. Placed on an existing concrete slab next to the house, a bed of compacted gravel, or on pavers as the shed in this project has been, moisture and freeze-thaw soil movement shouldn't be problems.

The design here is large enough to easily hold a large lidded garbage can and large recycling can side by side. You can scale down the design if you use smaller cans (or add shelves to one bay, if you use bins exclusively for your recycling). In any case, the design includes lids and doors so that you can move the cans out of the shed on trash day, and just pop garbage bags or recyclables into the cans at any other time.

A simple, rugged structure, this shed is meant to be easy to build and utilitarian, while still offering a visual upgrade on bare garbage and recycling cans cluttering your landscape.

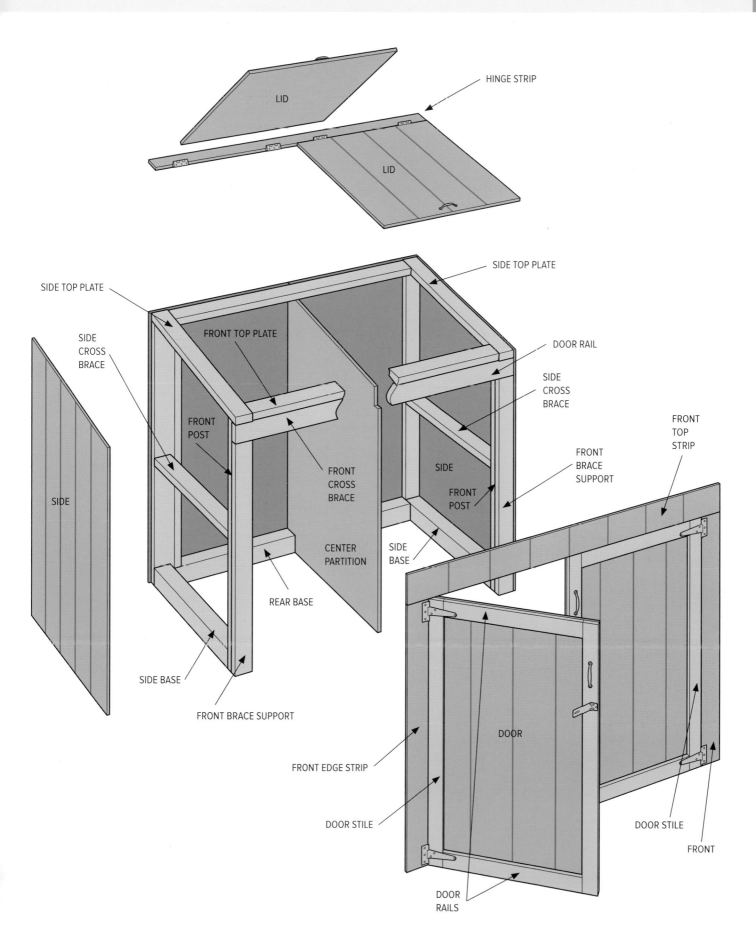

LID

LID

HINGE STRIP

SIDE TOP PLATE

SIDE TOP PLATE

FRONT TOP PLATE

DOOR RAIL

SIDE
CROSS
BRACE

SIDE
CROSS
BRACE

FRONT
POST

FRONT
TOP
STRIP

SIDE

FRONT
CROSS
BRACE

SIDE

FRONT
BRACE
SUPPORT

FRONT
POST

CENTER
PARTITION

SIDE
BASE

REAR BASE

SIDE
BASE

SIDE BASE

FRONT BRACE SUPPORT

DOOR

FRONT EDGE STRIP

DOOR STILE

DOOR STILE

FRONT

DOOR
RAILS

SHOPPING LIST

DESCRIPTION	QTY/SIZE	MATERIAL
FOUNDATION		
Drainage material	¾ yard	Compactible gravel
FRAME		
Side bases	2 @ 33½"	4 × 4 pressure treated
Rear base	1 @ 53"	4 × 4 pressure treated
Front posts	2 @ 46½"	2 × 4 pressure treated
Rear posts	4 @ 52½"	2 × 4 pressure treated
Side cross braces	2 @ 33½"	2 × 4 pressure treated
Side top plates	2 @ 38"	2 × 4 pressure treated
Front brace support	2 @ 43"	2 × 4 pressure treated
Front cross brace	2 @ 63"	2 × 4 pressure treated
Front & rear top plates	1 @ 56"	2 × 4 pressure treated
Center partition	1 @ 38" × 52½"	¾" exterior-grade plywood
CLADDING		
Sides	2 @ 38" × 54"	T1-11 siding
Rear	2 @ 31½" × 54"	T1-11 siding
Front edge strip	2 @ 4⅛" × 48"	T1-11 siding
Hinge strip	1 @ 3½" × 63"	T1-11 siding
Front top strip	1 @ 5" × 64¼"	T1-11 siding (2 pieces)
DOORS & LIDS		
Lids	2 @ 38" × 52½"	⅝" exterior-grade plywood
Doors	2 @ 28" × 46¼"	T1-11 siding
Door stiles	4 @ 41¼"	1 × 3 pine
Door rails	4 @ 23"	1 × 3 pine
HARDWARE		
Door hinges	4 @ 5"	Enameled T hinge
Lid hinges	4 @ 3"	Stainless steel door hinge
Handles	4 @ 3"	Sash handle
Catches	2	Cabinet friction catch
FASTENERS		
6" lag screws	4	
2½" wood screws	30	
3" wood screws	60	
6d galvanized finishing nails	100	
Construction adhesive	1 tube	

How to Build A Garbage & Recycling Shed

1

Choose a site for the shed (ideally, as close as possible to the kitchen or back door). If the site is not a concrete slab, it's best to create a stable, level surface for the shed. Here, an existing sand-set paver patio was refurbished and leveled for the shed.

2

Lay out all the sidewall pieces, measure and cut them for both walls. Mark the tops of the front and rear posts on each side for the angle of the top using a framing square.

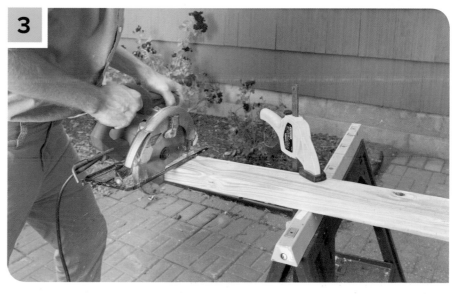

3

Make the cuts for all the sidewall pieces, the braces, and top caps. Assemble the side walls. The top caps will be longer than the outside faces of the front and rear posts.

4

Use a speed square to mark the angled cut on the front and back of the sidewall top caps. Make the mitered cuts with a jigsaw.

5

Cut the front cross brace supports and screw them in place on the front of each sidewall front post, leaving a 3½" space between the top of the support and the bottom of the top plate.

6

Lay one completed sidewall on top of the 1" plywood for the center partition. Use a 2 × 4 spacer to create a 1½" space between the bottom edge of the wall and the bottom edge of the plywood. Outline the shape of the sidewall onto the plywood, including the angled top cuts and the front and rear edge cuts. Remove the sidewall and cut the partition. Prime and paint or finish the partition, including the edges.

7

Screw the sidewalls to the rear base using countersunk 6" lag screws. Drive a lag screw through each of the rear wall posts and the side bases.

8

Stand a rear wall post face to edge against the sidewall rear post and use the sidewall post as a reference to mark the cut line on the top of the rear wall post. Assemble the rear wall by driving 3" screws through the posts into the ends of the 4 × 4 rear wall base. Screw the rear wall top plate to the posts with 3" wood screws driven down through the top plate and into the end grain of the posts.

9

Drive 3" wood screws through the faces of the rear wall posts into the sidewall rear posts' edges, every 6". Position the front cross brace in place, resting on the front brace supports, and screw it to the sidewall front posts with 2½" wood screws.

10

Mark the centerpoints of the front cross brace and the rear wall 4 × 4 base. Align the plywood partition wall in place with these centerpoints. Drill pilot holes and then nail the rear wall top plate and front cross brace to the edges of the plywood partition.

Position the 56"-long front top plate between the side top plates so the front edge is flush with the front edge of the front cross brace. Screw the front top plate to the front cross brace. Secure the ends of the top plate into each sidewall top plate with screws driven toenail-style from below.

Hold one 38" × 55" side-wall T1-11 panel against the sidewall frame with the ripped front and rear edges aligned with the sidewall front and rear edges. Screw the panel to the side wall, every 6" around the edges and every 10" in the field. Repeat with the opposite sidewall.

Use a jigsaw to cut the siding panels flush with the top face of both sidewall top rails. Nail two ripped-down panels on the rear wall, so the center seam aligns on the partition. Attach 3½" × 48" strips of ripped siding panel on either side of the front, using brads.

Cut the two lids from ⅝" exterior plywood, each 34½" by 31½". Rip the 3½" × 63" hinge strip from the same plywood. Coat the underside of the rear panel with construction adhesive, and use finish nails to fasten the rear panel across the rear top plate and sidewalls.

Paint or finish the lids if applying a top finish. Once dry, attach them to the rear top plate and plywood rear panel with two 3" door hinges per lid. Attach two 3" sash handles centered on the lids at the front edge.

Screw the front frame of 1 × 3 pine pieces around the front edges of the T1-11 door panels, driving the 1" wood screws from the inside of the doors. Mount the doors to the frame of the shed with 5" T-hinges, two per door. Install two friction catches for each door, one on either side of the plywood partition, and a slide-bolt latch on the doors.

CALLBOX SHED

Roughly the size of an old-fashioned phone booth or police call box, this shed is just large enough to store a group of long-handled yard tools and a few supplies. It's also ideally suited for quick and easy modification: add tool hangers on any of the three interior walls, or tack cleats to the sidewalls for one or more shelves.

The shed is designed to sit atop a gravel bed, but it could easily fit right into a discreet corner of a concrete patio. It can even be moved with the aid of one or two helpers, so that you can keep it in different parts of the yard or garden in different seasons, depending on what your needs are any given time of the year.

The door used is an understated siding panel reinforced with a cleat frame on the back. However, you could just as easily put the frame on the front and resize it to the outline of the door for a more conventional, attention-getting look. The design here includes a sliding bolt to keep the shed secure.

Designed roughly to the dimensions of an old-fashioned telephone booth, this shed has a remarkably useful interior space and a handsome appearance that would work well in any yard.

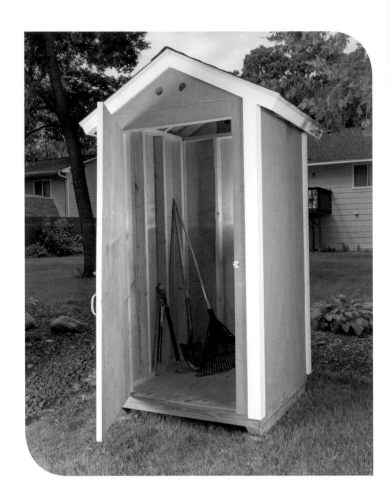

MATERIALS LIST

DESCRIPTION	QTY/SIZE	MATERIAL
FOUNDATION		
Crushed gravel	3 bags	
FRAMING & WALLS		
Skids	2 @ 48"	4 × 4 pressure treated
Floor joists	4 @ 45"	2 × 4 pressure treated
Floor rim joists	2 @ 48"	2 × 4 pressure treated
Floor	1 @ 48" × 48"	⅝" exterior grade
Sidewall studs	8 @ 80"	2 × 4
Front & rear wall studs	10 @ 80"	2 × 4
Front wall jack studs	2 @ 76½"	2 × 4
Front wall header	2 @ 39"	2 × 4
Front & rear top plate	2 @ 48"	2 × 4
Sidewall top plate	2 @ 41"	2 × 4
Sidewall sole plate	2 @ 41"	2 × 4

MATERIALS LIST (continued)

DESCRIPTION	QTY/SIZE	MATERIAL
FOUNDATION (continued)		
Rear wall sole plate	1 @ 48"	2 × 4
Front wall sole plate	2 @ 6"	2 × 4
Roof ridge board	1 @ 48"	2 × 4
Gable end stud	2 @ 9¾"	2 × 4
Rafter	8 @ 34¼"	2 × 4
Soffit trim	2 @ 51"	2 × 4
Gable trim	2 @ 48¾"	2 × 4
Roof sheathing	2 @ 35¾" × 51"	2 × 4
Corner trim	8 @ 3½" × 84"	1 × 4 pine
ROOF		
Drip edge	1 @ 35¾", 2 @ 51"	Galvanized metal
15# roofing paper	36 sq. ft.	
Shingles	⅓ square	Asphalt shingles
SIDING		
Side & rear wall siding	3 @ 48" × 84"	T1-11 siding
Front siding	2 @ 6" × 84", 1 @ 5" × 36"	T1-11 siding
Gable end siding	2 @ 13¼" × 48"	T1-11 siding
DOOR		
Door panel	1 @ 36" × 76½"	T1-11 siding
Frame stile	2 @ 72½"	1 × 3 cedar
Frame rail	3 @ 27"	1 × 3 cedar
FASTENERS & HARDWARE		
Z-flashing	2 @ 48"	
Construction adhesive	1 tube	
Silicone caulk	1 tube	
Door handle	1	5" sash, black
Strap hinges	3	4" black
Bolt lock	1	4"
3" deck screws	20	
2½" deck screws	½ lb.	
1" galvanized roofing nails	½ lb.	
8d galvanized siding nails	½ lb.	
Screening	1 linear foot	Black aluminum

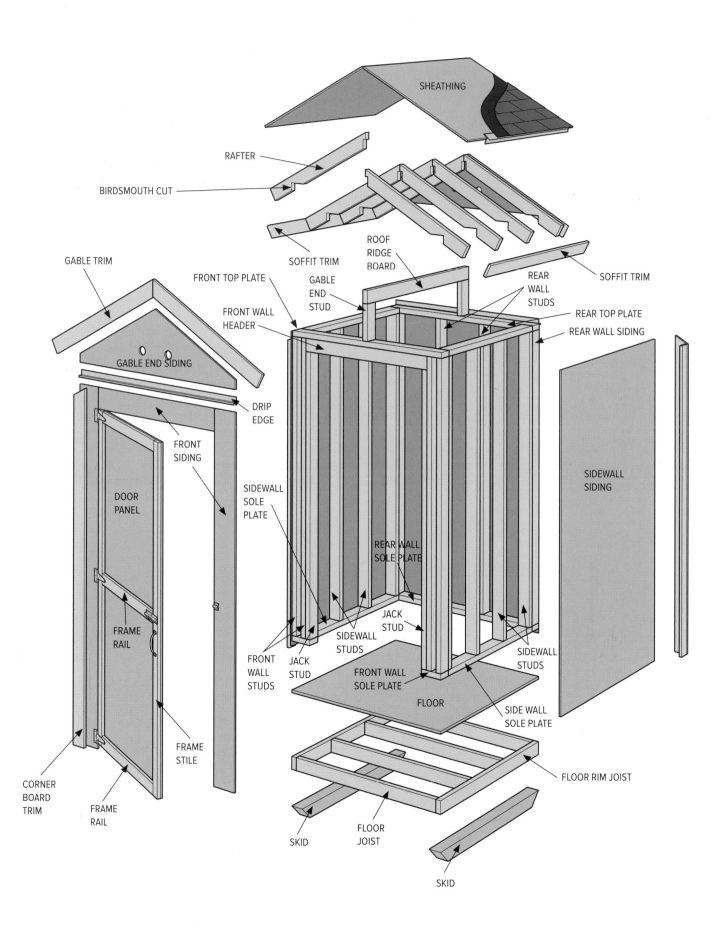

SHEATHING

RAFTER

BIRDSMOUTH CUT

SOFFIT TRIM

ROOF RIDGE BOARD

GABLE TRIM

FRONT TOP PLATE

GABLE END STUD

REAR WALL STUDS

SOFFIT TRIM

FRONT WALL HEADER

REAR TOP PLATE

REAR WALL SIDING

GABLE END SIDING

DRIP EDGE

FRONT SIDING

DOOR PANEL

SIDEWALL SOLE PLATE

SIDEWALL SIDING

REAR WALL SOLE PLATE

FRAME RAIL

JACK STUD

SIDEWALL STUDS

FRONT WALL STUDS

JACK STUD

FRONT WALL SOLE PLATE

SIDEWALL STUDS

CORNER BOARD TRIM

FRAME RAIL

FRAME STILE

FLOOR

SIDE WALL SOLE PLATE

FLOOR RIM JOIST

SKID

FLOOR JOIST

SKID

How to Build the Call Box Shed

1

**Prepare two parallel 4" deep × 4" wide × 50"
long trenches** (spaced 44" apart, on center). Fill them
with crushed gravel, and compact to a level surface.
Check for level between the trenches and along the
length of both, using a 4-foot carpenter's level. Clip
each end of the 4 × 4 skids to a 45-degree angle.
Center the skids on the trenches, 48" from one
outside face to the other.

2

On a flat work surface, lay out the floor frame, with the joists and rim joists on edge. Screw
the rim joists to the ends of each joist, using 3" deck screws. Center the floor frame on the
skids and toe screw the joists to the skids. Position the plywood floor on the frame so that all
edges are flush, and screw the floor to the frame with 2½" deck screws.

3

Build the first sidewall, screwing the top and sole
plates flush to the outside studs. Screw the inside
studs in place, spaced 13¼" on center. Build the
second sidewall in the same way. Brace them in place
on the floor, checking to make sure they that they are
plumb. Use the same method to build the rear wall,
but with double studs on the edges, and the inside
studs spaced 13½" on-center. Position the rear wall
on the floor, bracing them to the side walls.

Create the door header by sandwiching two 39" 2 × 4s together with construction adhesive and pairs of 2½" deck screws driven every 4". Center the header on the underside of the top plate and screw it in place using 3" deck screws driven down through the top plate. Screw the king studs to either side of the header, and to the top plate. Install the jack studs on the inside of the king studs. Screw the top plate to the outside front-wall studs, and screw the sole plates to the bottoms of the outside studs, king studs, and jack studs to complete the front wall.

Nail the sidewall sole plates through the floor and into the floor frame. Screw the sidewalls to the rear wall with 3" deck screws. Put the front wall in position, measure the diagonals to ensure square, and screw the sole plates to the floor and the side walls to the front wall.

Starting with the sidewalls, install the plywood siding panels. Side the rear wall, then cut the sections for the front wall and nail them in place.

Cut the rafters, including two rafters that are ¾" longer and have no birdsmouth cut. These will be the front and back trim pieces. Toenail the ridge board to the gable studs, and position the ridge board assembly on the top plates, front to back (centered side to side). Toenail the rafters to the top plates, and to the ridge board. The front and rear rafters should be flush with the outer edges of the top plates.

8

Install Z-flashing along the top plate on the gable ends and caulk the edge. Install the gable end plywood panels in place on the front and rear walls, and use a jigsaw to trim off the corners of the panel to match the slope of the end rafters. Use a 3" hole saw to drill two vent holes on either side of the gable end stud.

9

Use 2½" deck screws to attach the trim boards to the front and rear rafter faces, and along the rafter ends on both sides. Sheath the roof with ½" plywood sections, nailed every 6" along each rafter. Attach the metal drip edge along the eaves, and cover the roof with building paper. Then add the metal drip edge along the roof edge along both gable ends. Install the asphalt shingles, laying the courses to overlap at the ridge.

10

Nail the cleat frame to the back of the T1-11 door panel. Hang the door using 3" galvanized strap hinges. Install the handle and sliding bolt. Cut and fasten screening over the inside of the gable siding holes, using construction adhesive. Paint the shed.

Creating shade can be a challenge, especially around hard surfaces like this concrete patio. Awnings and sun sails and patio umbrellas can provide temporary solutions, but wind and the elements can diminish your enjoyment or even lead to minor disasters. If your outdoor living area is overly exposed to sun or wind, a pergola might be just the solution you need.

The four-post patio pergola shown here will withstand just about anything nature can throw at it, plus it adds warmth and architectural interest to a fairly plain setting. The pergola is typically understood as a freestanding, four-post structure supporting an arbor-type canopy and often used to train vining plants. The elements are simple: posts bases (metal or concrete), four wood posts, joists, and corbels that support a series of wood rafters running perpendicular to the joists; and often it is capped with thinner purlins running across the rafters to provide shade, trellising and visual interest.

The hardware system we chose to use for this pergola is from a relatively new line called Outdoor Accents®, manufactured and sold by joist-hanger giant Simpson Strong-Tie (See Resources, page 143). The powder-coat black bases, caps, hangers and fasteners have a very dramatic presence in the final design. But even though they look like they are fastened with typical heavy-duty lag screws, the beefy hex heads you see are actually washers for the primary fasteners: exterior wood screws that do not require pilot holes and can be driven easily by any drill-driver or impact driver, eliminating at least a couple of steps.

Containers of climbing plants such as clematis or ivy or Virginia creeper can be positioned at the bases of the posts, or you may choose to plant another vining plants—the homeowner where this structure was built intends to plant it with Cascade hops.

MATERIALS

2 × 2 × 8 feet for purlins (18)	post anchors (4)	*As shown:
4 × 4 × 8 feet for posts and corbels (6)	rafter ties (28)	Base = 7' 7½" wide × 9' 7½" deep
2 × 8 × 12 for joists (4)	3" exterior wood screws	Height: 8' 9½"
2 × 10 × 12 for rafters (7)	5½" wood screws with washers	
post base hardware (4)	3½" wood screws with washers	

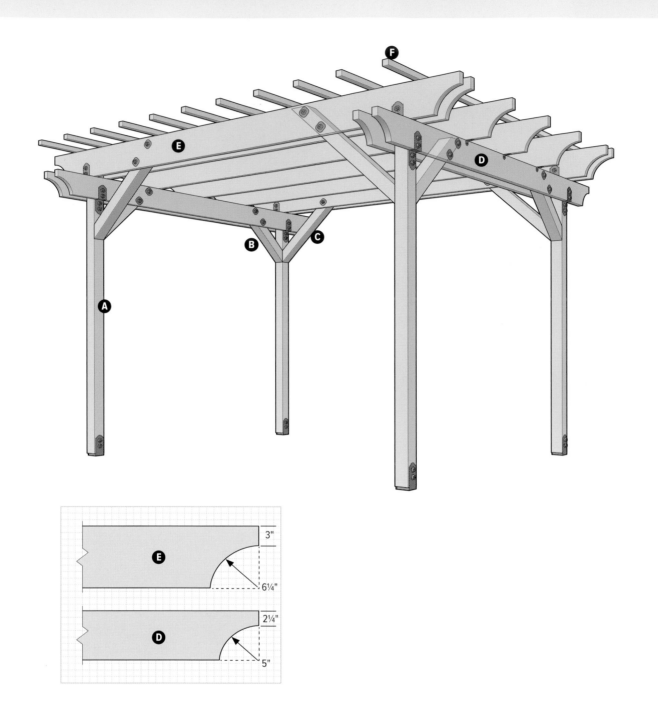

CUTTING LIST

KEY	QUANTITY	SIZE	PART	MATERIAL
A	4	3½" × 3½" × 104"	Post	Ext. lumber
B	4	3½" × 3½" × 30"	Corbel-front/back	Ext. lumber
C	4	3½" × 3½" × 43⁷⁄₁₆"	Corbel-side	Ext. lumber
D	4	1½" × 7¼" × 120"	Joist	Ext. lumber
E	7	1½" × 9¼" × 120"	Rafter	Ext. lumber
F	11	1½" × 1½" × 120"	Purlin	Ext. lumber

Four-Post Patio Pergola

Make templates for the joist end profiles (see page 126). Use a cutoff piece of the correct width board for each part and plot the end profile according to the diagram. Cut the profiles on the cutoff pieces with a jigsaw to make the templates. Trace onto the workpieces.

Smooth the cut end profiles with a sander and break the edges of the cuts into a slight bevel to help prevent splintering.

Lay a post/joist assembly in position on the surface and set post base hardware flush against the post ends. Trace the post base location onto the surface.

Tack the mating joist in position on the opposite sides of the posts from the first joist, using deck screws.

5

Drill guide holes for the post base anchors using a hammer drill and masonry bit.

6

After driving the anchor bolt into the guide hole, fasten down the pedestal bases for the first end post pair assembly. Install the post standoff platforms.

7

Erect the end-post assembly in the post bases, checking with a level to make sure the posts are plumb. Tack the posts temporarily to the bases with deck screws.

8

Drive the post base fasteners through the base saddles and into the post. Keep them slightly loose so you can still adjust the assembly later.

9

Double check that the posts are plumb and the joists are level. Attach the finished hardware for permanently connecting the joists and posts.

10

With both post assemblies secured, position and tack and outer rafter at each corner.

Finish driving the final fasteners at all post bases and check again for plumb and square.

Attach the finished rafter hardware to the outer rafter at each corner.

Clamp 4×4 stock across the corbel locations at each corner and transfer cutting lines where they cross the rafter tops. Remove the corbel stock and make the angled cuts with a power miter saw.

Make the angled cuts where the corbels meet the posts and then tack into position with deck screws.

When all the corbels are cut, aligned, and tacked into place, attach the final hardware.

Install the remaining rafters, using L-brackets to reinforce the joints.

Attach the purlins to the rafter tops with exterior screws driven from above.

FREESTANDING ARBOR

Create a shady retreat in a sunny yard with this striking cedar arbor. It can also support a wealth of climbing plants if you so choose.

This freestanding arbor combines the beauty and durability of natural cedar with an Asian-inspired design. Set it up on your patio or deck or in a quiet corner of your backyard. It adds just the right finishing touch to turn your outdoor living space into a showplace geared for relaxation and quiet contemplation.

The arbor has a long history as a focal point in gardens and other outdoor areas throughout the world. And if privacy and shade are concerns, you can enhance the sheltering quality by adding climbing vines that weave their way in and out of the trellis. Or, simply set a few potted plants around the base to help the arbor blend in with the outdoor environment, or hang potted plants from the top beams.

This arbor is freestanding, so it can be moved to a new site if you desire. Or, you can anchor it permanently to a deck or to the ground and equip it with a built-in seat. The curved cutouts that give the arbor its design appeal are made with a jigsaw.

TOOLS & MATERIALS

1" × 2" × 8 ft. cedar boards (7)
2" × 4" × 8 ft. cedar boards (9)
2" × 6" × 8 ft. cedar boards (3)
Wood glue (exterior)
Wood sealer or stain
#10 × 2½" wood screws
⅜"-dia. × 2½" lag screws (8)
6" lag screws (4)
Deck screws (2½", 3")

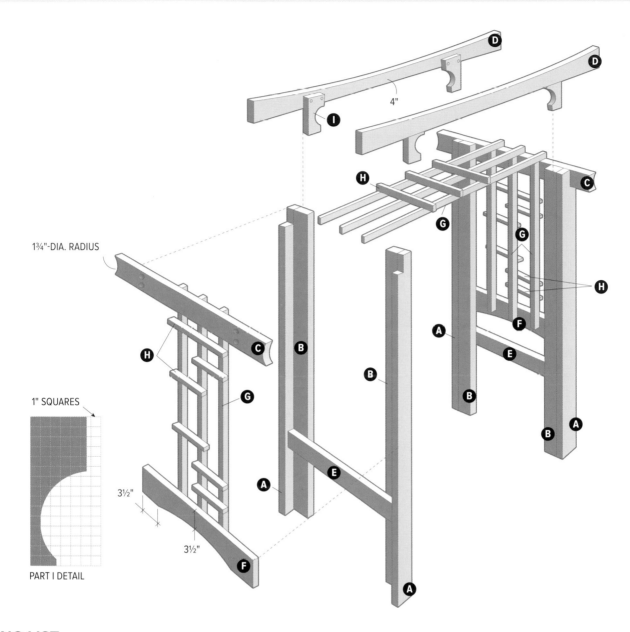

1¾"-DIA. RADIUS

1" SQUARES

3½"

3½"

PART I DETAIL

4"

CUTTING LIST

KEY	QUANTITY	SIZE	PART	MATERIAL
A	4	1½" × 3½" × 72"	Leg fronts	Cedar
B	4	1½" × 3½" × 72"	Leg sides	Cedar
C	2	1½" × 3½" × 36"	Cross beams	Cedar
D	2	1½" × 5½" × 72"	Top beams	Cedar
E	2	1½" × 3½" × 21"	Side rails	Cedar
F	2	1½" × 5½" × 21"	Side spreaders	Cedar
G	9	⅞" × 1½" × 48"	Trellis strips	Cedar
H	15	⅞" × 1½" × *	Cross strips	Cedar
I	4	1½" × 5½" × 15"	Braces	Cedar

*Cut to fit

How to Build the Freestanding Arbor

Create four leg pairs by fastening two 6-foot-long pieces of 2 × 4 cedar at right angles, with top and bottom edges flush, using 3" deck screws. Apply moisture-resistant glue to the joint, and try to keep your screw spacing uniform. Attach the leg fronts to the leg sides by driving evenly spaced screws through the faces of the fronts and into the edges of the sides.

Use a jigsaw to cut a 3½"-long × 1½"-wide notch (actual 2 × 4 dimensions) at the top outside corner of each leg front. These notches cradle the crossbeams when the arbor is assembled. Cut the crossbeams to length.

Lay out semicircle profiles on the ends of the crossbeams. Use a piece of cardboard as a template for tracing the arcs. Draw a 3½"-diameter semicircle at the edge of the cardboard strip and cut out the semicircle for the template. Cut out the arcs on the workpieces with a jigsaw. Sand smooth with a drill and drum sander attachment. Also cut two side spreaders to length.

Drill ⅜"-diameter pilot holes in the crossbeams and attach them to the legs with two ⅜"-diameter × 2½" lag screws and glue. Fasten the spreaders and rails with deck screws to assemble the side frames.

HOW TO MAKE A TRAMMEL

The long, gentle curves on the side spreaders and top beams can be laid out with a makeshift trammel. For example, to mark the cutting lines on the side spreaders, draw starting points 3½" in from each end of a spreader (see diagram, page 133). Make a reference line 2" up from the bottom of the spreader board. For the top beams, draw 1½"-deep arcs at the top edges of the top beams, starting at the ends of each of the boards to lay out your curves.

Tack a casing nail at the peaks of the reference lines. Also tack nails into the workpiece next to the starting point for each arc. Slip a thin strip of metal or plastic between the casing nails so the strip bows out to create a smooth arc. Trace the arc onto the workpiece, then cut along the line with a jigsaw. Smooth with a drum sander. Use the first part of each type as a template for marking and cutting the second, matching part.

5

6

Cut the trellis strips and cross strips to length from 1 × 2 cedar. Attach the 48"-long vertical trellis strips to the crossbeams and spreaders, spaced 2⅜" apart, with the ends flush with the top of the crossbeam. Use 2½" deck screws driven through pilot holes.

Brace the side frames in an upright, level position with long pieces of 1 × 4 while you attach the top beams. Clamp the ends of the braces to the side frames so the side frames are 4 feet apart, and use a level to make sure the side frames are plumb. Secure the top beams to the crossbeams with 6" lag screws, 12¾" from each end of each top beam.

> ### *WHERE TO PUT YOUR ARBOR*
> *There are no firm rules about arbor placement. It can be positioned to provide a focal point for a porch, patio, or deck. Placed against a wall or at the end of a plain surface, arbors improve the general look of the area. With some thick climbing vines and vegetation added to the arbor, you can also disguise a utility area, such as a trash collection space.*

7

Temporarily lock the legs in a square position for transport after assembling the arbor by tacking strips of wood between the front legs and between the back legs.

8

Cut the cross strips to 7" and 10" lengths. Use wood screws driven into pilot holes to attach them at 3" intervals in a staggered pattern on the side trellis pieces. You can adjust the sizes and placement of the cross strips but, for best appearance, retain some symmetry of placement. Fasten cross strips to the top trellis in the same manner. To protect the arbor, coat the cedar wood with clear wood sealer. After the finish dries, the arbor is ready to be placed onto your deck or patio or in a quiet corner of your yard.

OPTION: ADD A SEAT

Create an arbor seat by resting two 2 × 10 cedar boards on the rails in each side frame. Overhang the rails by 6" or so, and drive a few 3" deck screws through the boards and into the rails to secure the seat. If you do this, also be sure to secure your arbor to the ground or deck/ patio surface.

FIREWOOD SHELTER

Stacks of firewood will stay drier and be less of an eyesore if you build this rustic firewood shelter.

This handsome firewood shelter combines rustic ranch styling with ample sheltered storage that keeps firewood off the ground and obscured from sight. Clad on the sides and roof with beveled cedar lap siding, the shelter has the look and feel of a permanent structure. But because it's freestanding, you can move it around as needed. It requires no time-consuming foundation work. As long as it's loaded up with firewood it is very stable, even in high winds. But if it has high exposure to the elements and is frequently empty, secure it with a pair of wood stakes.

This firewood shelter is large enough to hold an entire face cord of firewood. (A face cord, also called a rick, is 4 feet high, 8 feet wide, and one log-length deep— typically 16".) Since the storage area is sheltered and raised to avoid ground contact and allow airflow, wood dries quickly and is ready to use when you need it. Raising the firewood above the ground also makes the woodpile a much less attractive nesting area for rodents.

TOOLS & MATERIALS

2" × 4" × 8' cedar boards (10)
2" × 6" × 8' cedar boards (5)
⅝" × 8" × 8' cedar lap siding (10)
⅜" × 3½" lag screws (24)
⅜" × 4" lag screws (8)
1½" spiral siding nails
Deck screws (2½", 3")
Finishing materials

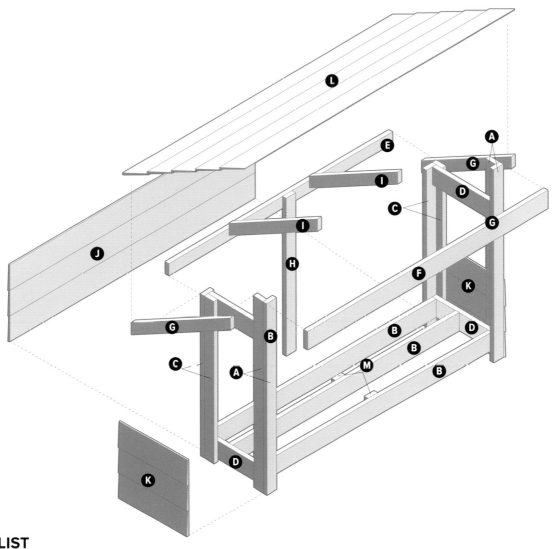

CUTTING LIST

KEY	QUANTITY	SIZE	PART	MATERIAL
A	4	1½" × 3½" × 59"	Front posts	Cedar
B	3	1½" × 5½" × 82½"	Bottom rails	Cedar
C	4	1½" × 3½" × 50"	Rear posts	Cedar
D	4	1½" × 5½" × 21"	End rails	Cedar
E	1	1½" × 3½" × 88½"	Back rail	Cedar
F	1	1½" × 5½" × 88½"	Front rail	Cedar
G	2	1½" × 3½" × 33¾"	Roof supports	Cedar
H	1	1½" × 3½" × 50"	Middle post	Cedar
I	2	1½" × 3½" × 28"	Middle supports	Cedar
J	3	⅝" × 8" × 88½"	Back siding	Cedar siding
K	6	⅝" × 8" × 24"	End siding	Cedar siding
L	5	⅝" × 8" × 96"	Roof strips	Cedar siding
M	2	1½" × 3½" × 7½"	Prop	Cedar

How to Build a Firewood Shelter

Cut the bottom rails and end rails. Assemble two bottom rails and two end rails into a rectangular frame, with the end rails covering the ends of the bottom rails. Center the third bottom rail between the end rails. Attach the end rails to the bottom rails with two ⅜" × 4" lag screws, with washers, driven into counterbored pilot holes.

Cut the front posts and rear posts to length. Join them into pairs with 2½" deck screws (see diagram, page 139). On a flat surface, set the rail assembly between the posts on 2" spacers. Drive a pair of ⅜" × 4" lag screws, fitted with washers, through the sides of the corner posts and into the bottom rails. Complete the frame by installing end rails at the tops of the corner posts.

Cut the back rail, front rail, roof supports, middle post, and middle supports to length. The roof supports and middle supports are mitered at the ends. To make the miter cutting lines, mark a point 1½" in from each end, along the edge of the board. Draw diagonal lines from each point to the opposing corner. Cut along the lines with a circular saw or power miter saw.

Attach the front and back rails by driving 3" deck screws through the outer roof supports, making sure the top of the rail is flush with the tops of the supports. The supports should overhang the posts equally in the front and rear.

Attach the middle supports by driving 3" deck screws through the rails and into the ends of the middle supports. The tops of the rails should be flush with the tops of the roof supports. Use a pipe clamp to hold the supports in place as you attach them. Install the middle post with 2½" deck screws so it extends 2" past the bottom rail. Attach one prop to the front and back rails.

Cut pieces of 8"-wide beveled cedar lap siding to length to make the siding strips and the roof strips. Starting 2" up from the bottoms of the rear posts, fasten the back siding strips. Work your way up, overlapping each piece of siding by ½", making sure the thicker edges of the siding face down. Attach the roof strips to the roof supports, starting at the back edge. Make sure the wide edge of the siding faces down. Attach the rest of the roof strips, overlapping the strip below by about ½". Apply wood sealer/finish if you wish.

Metric Conversions

TO CONVERT:	TO:	MULTIPLY BY:
Inches	Millimeters	25.4
Inches	Centimeters	24.5
Feet	Meters	0.305
Yards	Meters	0.914
Square inches	Square centimeters	6.45
Square feet	Square meters	0.093
Square yards	Square meters	0.836
Ounces	Milliliters	30.0
Pints (U.S.)	Liters	0.473 (Imp. 0.568)
Quarts (U.S.)	Liters	0.946 (Imp. 1.136)
Gallons (U.S.)	Liters	3.785 (Imp. 4.546)
Ounces	Grams	28.4
Pounds	Kilograms	0.454

TO CONVERT:	TO:	MULTIPLY BY:
Millimeters	Inches	0.039
Centimeters	Inches	0.394
Meters	Feet	3.28
Meters	Yards	1.09
Square centimeters	Square inches	0.155
Square meters	Square feet	10.8
Square meters	Square yards	1.2
Milliliters	Ounces	.033
Liters	Pints (U.S.)	2.114 (Imp. 1.76)
Liters	Quarts (U.S.)	1.057 (Imp. 0.88)
Liters	Gallons (U.S.)	0.264 (Imp. 0.22)
Grams	Ounces	0.035
Kilograms	Pounds	2.2

Converting Temperatures

Convert degrees Fahrenheit (F) to degrees Celsius (C) by following this simple formula: Subtract 32 from the Fahrenheit temperature reading. Then, multiply that number by $\frac{5}{9}$. For example, 77°F - 32 = 45. 45 $\times$ $\frac{5}{9}$ = 25°C.

To convert degrees Celsius to degrees Fahrenheit, multiply the Celsius temperature reading by $\frac{9}{5}$. Then, add 32. For example, 25°C $\times$ $\frac{9}{5}$ = 45. 45 + 32 = 77°F.

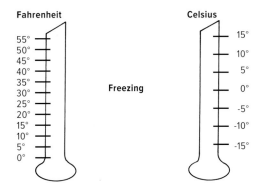

Metric Plywood Panels

Metric plywood panels are commonly available in two sizes: 1,200 mm $\times$ 2,400 mm and 1,220 mm $\times$ 2,400 mm, which is roughly equivalent to a 4 $\times$ 8-ft. sheet. Standard and Select sheathing panels come in standard thicknesses, while Sanded grade panels are available in special thicknesses.

STANDARD SHEATHING GRADE		SANDED GRADE	
7.5 mm	($\frac{5}{16}$ in.)	6 mm	($\frac{4}{17}$ in.)
9.5 mm	($\frac{3}{8}$ in.)	8 mm	($\frac{5}{16}$ in.)
12.5 mm	($\frac{1}{2}$ in.)	11 mm	($\frac{7}{16}$ in.)
15.5 mm	($\frac{5}{8}$ in.)	14 mm	($\frac{9}{16}$ in.)
18.5 mm	($\frac{3}{4}$ in.)	17 mm	($\frac{2}{3}$ in.)
20.5 mm	($\frac{13}{16}$ in.)	19 mm	($\frac{3}{4}$ in.)
22.5 mm	($\frac{7}{8}$ in.)	21 mm	($\frac{13}{16}$ in.)
25.5 mm	(1 in.)	24 mm	($\frac{15}{16}$ in.)

Lumber Dimensions

NOMINAL - U.S.	ACTUAL - U.S. (IN INCHES)	METRIC
1 $\times$ 2	$\frac{3}{4}$ $\times$ 1$\frac{1}{2}$	19 $\times$ 38 mm
1 $\times$ 3	$\frac{3}{4}$ $\times$ 2$\frac{1}{2}$	19 $\times$ 64 mm
1 $\times$ 4	$\frac{3}{4}$ $\times$ 3$\frac{1}{2}$	19 $\times$ 89 mm
1 $\times$ 5	$\frac{3}{4}$ $\times$ 4$\frac{1}{2}$	19 $\times$ 114 mm
1 $\times$ 6	$\frac{3}{4}$ $\times$ 5$\frac{1}{2}$	19 $\times$ 140 mm
1 $\times$ 7	$\frac{3}{4}$ $\times$ 6$\frac{1}{4}$	19 $\times$ 159 mm
1 $\times$ 8	$\frac{3}{4}$ $\times$ 7$\frac{1}{4}$	19 $\times$ 184 mm
1 $\times$ 10	$\frac{3}{4}$ $\times$ 9$\frac{1}{4}$	19 $\times$ 235 mm
1 $\times$ 12	$\frac{3}{4}$ $\times$ 11$\frac{1}{4}$	19 $\times$ 286 mm
1$\frac{1}{4}$ $\times$ 4	1 $\times$ 3$\frac{1}{2}$	25 $\times$ 89 mm
1$\frac{1}{4}$ $\times$ 6	1 $\times$ 5$\frac{1}{2}$	25 $\times$ 140 mm
1$\frac{1}{4}$ $\times$ 8	1 $\times$ 7$\frac{1}{4}$	25 $\times$ 184 mm
1$\frac{1}{4}$ $\times$ 10	1 $\times$ 9$\frac{1}{4}$	25 $\times$ 235 mm
1$\frac{1}{4}$ $\times$ 12	1 $\times$ 11$\frac{1}{4}$	25 $\times$ 286 mm
1$\frac{1}{2}$ $\times$ 4	1$\frac{1}{4}$ $\times$ 3$\frac{1}{2}$	32 $\times$ 89 mm
1$\frac{1}{2}$ $\times$ 6	1$\frac{1}{4}$ $\times$ 5$\frac{1}{2}$	32 $\times$ 140 mm
1$\frac{1}{2}$ $\times$ 8	1$\frac{1}{4}$ $\times$ 7$\frac{1}{4}$	32 $\times$ 184 mm
1$\frac{1}{2}$ $\times$ 10	1$\frac{1}{4}$ $\times$ 9$\frac{1}{4}$	32 $\times$ 235 mm
1$\frac{1}{2}$ $\times$ 12	1$\frac{1}{4}$ $\times$ 11$\frac{1}{4}$	32 $\times$ 286 mm
2 $\times$ 4	1$\frac{1}{2}$ $\times$ 3$\frac{1}{2}$	38 $\times$ 89 mm
2 $\times$ 6	1$\frac{1}{2}$ $\times$ 5$\frac{1}{2}$	38 $\times$ 140 mm
2 $\times$ 8	1$\frac{1}{2}$ $\times$ 7$\frac{1}{4}$	38 $\times$ 184 mm
2 $\times$ 10	1$\frac{1}{2}$ $\times$ 9$\frac{1}{4}$	38 $\times$ 235 mm
2 $\times$ 12	1$\frac{1}{2}$ $\times$ 11$\frac{1}{4}$	38 $\times$ 286 mm
3 $\times$ 6	2$\frac{1}{2}$ $\times$ 5$\frac{1}{2}$	64 $\times$ 140 mm
4 $\times$ 4	3$\frac{1}{2}$ $\times$ 3$\frac{1}{2}$	89 $\times$ 89 mm
4 $\times$ 6	3$\frac{1}{2}$ $\times$ 5$\frac{1}{2}$	89 $\times$ 140 mm

Liquid Measurement Equivalents

1 Pint	= 16 Fluid Ounces	= 2 Cups
1 Quart	= 32 Fluid Ounces	= 2 Pints
1 Gallon	= 128 Fluid Ounces	= 4 Quarts

RESOURCES

TOOLS, MATERIALS & GEAR
Black & Decker (US), Inc.
800 544 6986
www.blackanddecker.com

WALKWAYS, PATIOS & DECKS
American Society of Landscape Architects
www.asla.org

The Brick Industry Association
www.gobrick.com

Portland Cement Association
www.cement.org

AZEK Building Products
www.azek.com

Belgard Hardscapes
www.belgard.com

Borgert Products, Inc.
www.borgertproducts.com

Common Ground Alliance
"Call Before You Dig"
811
www.call811.com

Quikrete
www.quikrete.com

WALLS & FENCES
California Redwood Association
www.calredwood.org

The Masonry Society
www.masonrysociety.org

National Concrete Masonry Association
www.ncma.org

Southern Pine Council
www.southernpine.com

PLAY & ENTERTAINMENT
National Program for Playground Safety
www.playgroundsafety.org

Consumer Product Safety Commission
www.cpsc.gov

SwingWorks
www.swingworks.com

Safe Kids
www.safekids.org

Playgrounds & Playground Equipment
www.playstarinc.com

Detailed Play Systems
www.detailedplay.com

Swingsetmall.com
www.swingsetmall.com

Swing Kingdom
www.swingkingdom.com

CedarWorks
www.cedarworks.com

RubberScapes
www.rubberscapes.net

Surface America
www.surfaceamerica.com

GameTime
www.gametime.com

SHEDS & STRUCTURES
Asphalt Roofing Manufacturers Association
www.asphaltroofing.org

Finley Products, Inc.
www.2x4basics.com

Simpson Strong-Tie Co.
www.strongtie.com

Arrow Storage Products
www.arrowsheds.com

Best Barns
www.bettersheds.com

Cedarshed Industries
www.cedarshed.com

Jamaica Cottage Shop
www.jamaicacottageshop.com

Lifetime Products
www.lifetime.com

Outdoor Living Today
www.outdoorlivingtoday.com

Reeds Ferry Small Buildings, Inc.
www.reedsferry.com

Summerwood Products
www.summerwood.com

Suncast Homeplace Collection
www.suncast.com/homeplace-collection

Tuff Shed
www.tuffshed.com

INDEX

INDEX